Through Crisis
To Freedom

DEDICATION

With gratitude to my parents, who have been supportive beyond understanding.

To Phillip, Howard and Dorothy, Gerry, and Cullen for their encouragement and work with the manuscript.

To Pat for her illustrations and typing and so much more.

And to all those who have shared their stories with me and encouraged me in living out my own story.

Through Crisis To Freedom

Bill Cane, Ph.D.

ACTA
Chicago Illinois

SOURCE NOTES

We thank the following publishers for permission to quote from these works:
1. Casteneda, Carlos, p. 1. *The Teachings of Don Juan*, New York: Ballantine.
2. Eliot, T. S., p. 32. *The Cocktail Party*, (pp. 364-365), *The Complete Plays and Poems*, New York: Harcourt, Brace, Jovanovich.
3. Nin, Anais, p. 81. *The House of Incest* (p. 56), Chicago, Swallow Press.
4. Bruner, Jerome S., p. 102. *On Knowing — Essays for the Left Hand* (p. 18). New York: Atheneum.

ACKNOWLEDGEMENTS

Kazantzakis, Nikos, *Report to Greco*, Bantam Books, N.Y. 1966.
Bateson, Gregory, *Steps to an Ecology of Mind*, Ballantine Books, N.Y., 1975.
Lonergan, Bernard, *Collection*, ed. by F. E. Crowe, Herder and Herder, 1967.
Berdyaev, Nicolas, *The Destiny of Man*, Harper and Row, N.Y., 1960.
Arendt, Hannah, *The Human Condition*, University of Chicago Press, 1958.

Library of Congress Catalog No. 79-89874
ISBN-0-914070-14-2

Printed in the United States of America

Preface

In my years of trying to minister to people, I have often felt the intense suffering of people who have faced personal crisis. I know for myself the anxiety of facing change. In each crisis instance, I looked for words to encourage, uplift, or strengthen the person in pain. Over the years, I began to see that crisis—illness, the death of a loved one, the loss of a job, financial trouble, separation, loneliness, divorce, or the like—is not so much an external calamity as it is a part of the internal and personal process of change and growth.

When I discovered Bill Cane's book, I saw in it a tool for helping people grow through crisis to a new personal freedom. The book accurately describes the steps in crisis situations. It uses a combination of stories from real life, summaries, and evocative drawings to help the reader identify the circumstances of crisis.

I began to identify with the people in the book, and I saw how my own growth and change was like theirs. In a way, Bill Cane's work is a "self-help" book. It is, however, a self-help book with a difference. By means of the creative exercises that have been provided by Cullen Schippe, this book invites you to join in the process. You are asked to go step-by-step through this book in order to get in touch with crisis in your own life.

It is with pride and pleasure that I offer this book to you. It is my fervent hope that you can use this book to help you discover your own experiences and your own inner resources. Understanding those experiences and using those resources, you can grow through crisis to freedom.

—GERARD P. WEBER, *President, ACTA*

Contents

Introduction

A few years ago, I met Manual. We needed water on our land and could not get it from the city. A neighbor brought Manuel over. I can still see him climbing out of the truck with a wire that looked like a car antenna clutched in his hand. He was old and he walked with a limp, but his eyes were bright and blue and sparkling. I had never met a "witcher" or diviner before.

Manual walked the land slowly, dragging one leg behind him, the wire held tightly in his hand. I followed him, curious and excited. I wanted to believe in what he was doing, but I was skeptical. For a long time we walked in silence and nothing happened. Then, suddenly, the wire began to twitch. "Here's water," Manual said. And he used a heavy copper wire to estimate its depth.

I helped a neighbor dig our well on the spot Manual chose. We had an old rig and progress was slow. Twenty feet one day, twenty-four the next, and so it went. We dug *past* the depth Manuel had estimated, and my spirits dropped. I kept hoping the next scoop of earth would reveal water. I felt desperate when it didn't.

When we finally hit water, it was sudden and unexpected — a surprise breaking in at the last moment. We lowered a pump into the hole. A geyser of water began spouting out of the pipe, and we ran our hands through it and rubbed our faces. I wanted to jump up and down and shout for joy.

Since that time, I have gone out witching wells with Manuel a number of times. People call him, as they have for forty years now, and he goes out and walks their land and locates water. Manuel never knows where the water is beforehand. He just climbs out of the truck and starts limping along, waiting, trusting that when he gets to the right spot something will let him know. Manuel has become for me a symbol of people searching — people in transition seeking what is right for them.

When any of us enters a period of transition in life, we cannot know beforehand how to begin looking for the new or where the new might be. We just have to begin limping along, trusting that when we reach the right place, we will know it somehow.

This book is for people who have entered or are entering a time of transition, change, or uncertainty — a time of sensing that things can no longer be the way they used to be. It is for seekers, for people who sense there is something more for them in life, but are not sure where to find it.

The book describes, step by step, the process of crisis, change, and exploration. It draws heavily upon the experience of people who have moved through crisis creatively. It tells the story of human beings at their best as they move through life changes. It describes steps others have taken and then asks, "Is this the way it is with you?" It describes possibilities others have uncovered and asks, "Might possibilities like these also be yours?" Whenever you are going through a process of change and human decision and your next steps are not clear to you, the book can be helpful.

Through Crisis To Freedom

It is not meant to be an answer book but a guide to help you along the way. It concentrates on *approaches* for your journey. In this sense, you will find one part missing — your journey—the part that only you can fill in. There are previews before each part of the book and response sections at the conclusion of each chapter. They are meant to help you trace the steps in your own process of change. Don't skip over them. Use them. Place *yourself* in the book.

One way to use the book is with a group. There is a great value to people gathering to share their journeys. They encourage each other and a camaraderie develops. Some difficult steps become less lonely when a person is aware that others are taking the same sort of steps. The guide sections provide ways for the members of a group to share their experiences.

Another way to use the book is by yourself. Linda, who was at a lonely point in her life when she read the manuscript, told me that the people in the book became her friends, friends who understood. She used it by herself, but she was not alone.

The guide sections can be used alone or shared with a friend, counselor, or spiritual director.

One word of clarification: The words *crisis* and *transition in life* sound momentous, beyond everyday experience. "Nothing that earth-shattering is happening with me." Actually misunderstandings, hurts, sickness, problems at work, tension in the family, uncertainty about the future, a vague dissatisfaction with life — all are indications of crisis. All demand a response from us and face us with decisions. Our responses and decisions *are* momentous, because how we respond and how we decide are slowly determining the direction of our journeys.

PART ONE

Paths Ending

You must always keep in mind that a path is only a path; if you feel you should not follow it, you must not stay with it under any conditions . . . There is no affront, to oneself or to others, in dropping it if that is what your heart is telling you to do . . .

Does this path have a heart?

If it does, the path is good; if it doesn't, it is of no use. Both paths lead nowhere; but one has a heart, the other doesn't. One makes for a joyful journey; as long as you follow it, you are one with it. The other will make you curse your life.

— CARLOS CASTANEDA, The Teachings of Don Juan

RECOGNIZING CRISIS

There are in life some predictable crises — definite states which everyone seems to go through. There are also unpredictable crises — paths which suddenly end:

- A relationship becomes shaky.
- Someone close dies.
- Work begins to take more and more out of the worker.
- Sickness strikes.
- Trust is lost.
- Communication breaks down.

Sometimes, no one event signals the ending of a path — only feelings of anxiety and depression, a sense that all is not right. Whenever something which has worked before ceases to work and there is nothing to take its place, a person enters a time of transition.

Most people have not been adequately prepared for transitions in life. Most have been brought up to fear crisis and to pretend it isn't there. When, in the course of my work, I ask people to describe a time of crisis in their lives, they often begin by saying that their lives have been ordinary. They really haven't had any profound experiences of paths ending. When pressed, however, they begin to describe events which have had enormous importance and have deeply influenced the course of their lives.

Many people carry times of hurt with them for years. Just recently, a man told me that he really could not recall any crises in his life. Maybe, he added, it was because his parents both died when he was very young. He had to learn then to live independently. For him, great crisis had come early, and he did not recognize it as such.

FACING THE FACT

Many people shy away from facing paths that are ending because they equate going through transitions with *having problems*. They feel that life should go smoothly and that there is something wrong if it does not. This is unfortunate. The times which do not go smoothly are the *growth* times—the times which make us truly human. It is during these periods of trial and change that a person's greatness can become apparent.

People who face crisis and enter the struggle to change are *heroic* in the root sense of the word. The Greek poets used the word *hero* to describe someone who left the humdrum of everyday life and entered a great and important conflict—war, love, search, rescue, and the like.

For the ancient Greeks, both the winners and the losers qualified as heroes because all alike had entered a struggle. There was a story that could be told about each of them. Only the non-participants failed to reach hero status.

The opportunity for heroism in our lives most often presents itself in the form of personal crisis. It is in facing the fact of crisis and in facing crisis itself that we depart the dull round of ordinary existence and begin to create our own stories.

PREVIEW

In this first part of the book, you will be learning how to recognize and face the fact that paths might be ending in your life. It is important for you to look at your own life and your own experiences. It is important, too, that you become accustomed to expressing and sharing those experiences. The Preview section of each part will help you enter the process of the following chapters. Answer these preview questions as frankly and clearly as you can. The answers you provide will be the source of much thought and much recognition throughout the next four chapters.

1. List five times in your life when you were learning something new (entering high school, your first job, falling in love, and the like). Try to express these experiences in a complete sentence.

   a. _____

   _____

   b. _____

   _____

   c. _____

   _____

   d. _____

   _____

   e. _____

   _____

2. Now choose one of the events you have listed. Describe it in some detail, answering the following questions:

   a. How did you feel about it?

   _____

   _____

   _____

   _____

   b. What did you do?

   _____

   _____

   _____

   _____

   c. How did you cope?

   _____

   _____

   _____

   _____

   d. How did you feel when the experience was over?

   _____

   _____

   _____

   _____

   e. What did you learn from the experience?

   _____

   _____

   _____

   _____

   f. How were you changed by the experience?

   _____

   _____

   _____

   _____

NOTE: *If you are using this book in a group or guided experience, it is important that these answers be shared. They ought not be challenged at this point. What is valuable is that you share the experience as you perceive it today.*

1 Crisis: Danger and Opportunity

Man's soul seems to have somehow grown bigger.
It can no longer fit within the old molds.

— NIKOS KAZANTZAKIS

WHAT IS CRISIS?

The word *crisis* is misleading. Suicide, drugs, disaster—
those are crises. People in hospitals are put on the "critical" list. Crisis is bad news—an experience to be avoided
at all costs.

The Chinese word for "crisis" gives a truer picture. It
consists of *two* ideograms—one is *danger*; the other is *opportunity*. English seems to stress the danger and minimize
the opportunity. Crisis is a time of change, a time of decision where something of life-and-death importance hangs
in the balance.

There is a tendency to approach people in crisis as if
they were sick. This tendency treats crisis as a disease. It is
as if people in crisis need help from normal people to bring
them back to where they belong. Crisis is, however, an
extraordinary opportunity for growth, a time when it becomes possible to break out of old molds that are no longer
nourishing. The dead-ends and cul-de-sacs in life can be
turning points—preludes to needed change.

People break with past patterns only when they have to; if there were no experiences of dead-end and frustration, no one might ever reach out to the new. The unexpected, the birth of the new, the interruption of the "same dull round" all keep lives from ruin and give hope.

The people described in this book all passed through crisis. They came to points in their lives at which the old answers no longer worked, and they were afraid. They found themselves in a sort of "no man's land." They no longer fit into the old molds, and yet there were no new molds that they could pour themselves into. They were tempted to turn back, to become adjusted, to copy the lives of others around them. But ultimately they found that they could not remain true to themselves that way.

So each of them chose, in one way or another, to move ahead, to live beyond his or her own background, and to fashion a different reality for themselves. In fear and trembling, without knowing *how* to do so beforehand, they each broke out of old molds and created new patterns which may have been unusual but at least were *sane*.

A young woman seated on the lawn was filled with anxiety and asked, "How will the new blades of grass know how to grow?" In her reverie she had touched a mystery often taken for granted: the process of change—how growth happens in fragile times and against overwhelming odds.

In crisis, you are somehow enabled to get in touch with sources of life deep inside yourself—sources you never knew were there. And then, mysteriously, like the blade of grass, you begin to know how to grow.

RESPONSE

At the end of each section in this text, you will have the opportunity to reflect and respond to the material. Handle the response material before you go on to the next section.

1. Describe a crisis you have experienced—a disruption that took place in your life.

   _____

   _____

   _____

   _____

   _____

2. Describe the changes which the crisis caused.

   _____

   _____

   _____

   _____

3. Describe how you felt about those changes.

   _____

   _____

   _____

   _____

2 *Cracks in a Secure World*

At the times of greatest change in our lives, we do not *understand* what is happening to us. It is seldom clear to us *at the time* even that we are entering a period of transition. All that is clear to us is that we feel unsettled, confused. What used to work for us no longer does so. There are the times when cracks appear in what was perceived to be a secure world, and that world becomes shaky.

For years, Larry had been a man in uniform—the tall, trim, commanding presence you see on a Navy recruiting poster. He had been a Catholic seminarian, a navy pilot, a pilot for Pan Am, and a member of the CIA.

His present life is a sharp contrast to his past. When I went to interview him, he was in spattered Levis, sitting at a potter's wheel in his garage. The neighborhood was integrated—he and his wife wanted their children to experience racial differences.

His decision to leave Pan Am and do pottery was a shock for some people, a delight for others. The street artists in San Francisco invariably knew him or knew of

him, "Oh yeah, I know him—the guy who used to fly for
Pan Am.'"
  I asked Larry what led him to make such a move. He
told me that decisions in his life had been the same for a
long time. From the nun who was his teacher in the sixth
grade, to his commander in the Navy, to the CIA, his
attitude toward authority had remained unchanged. Larry
was not sure when the change began, but he remembered
a moment that seemed very significant.

  Some guys at the time whom I characterized as long-
  haired, dirty, hippie bums came around passing out
  leaflets about the Vietnam war, and they gave me one
  and kept going. The one who handed it to me really
  repelled me. I took the thing so as not to cause a
  scene. The leaflet was really persuasive about our role
  in the Vietnam war. I started to question things. A
  little later, I made a cursillo, and these things began to
  dove-tail. For the first time I really questioned authority. I got to a point where I recognized that authority
  was really a lot less important than my own attitude
  toward things.

  Larry grew up seeking circles of security. He was a person responsive to authority and to group pressure. He
wanted desparately to be identified with the team. In college he was "Mr. Active" and was elected to political office
at the school.

  When I got out of college, I went into the navy to
  become a pilot because that was the kind of thing that
  gives a person identity.
    Going into the navy and working for a military
  superior and doing a good job was no different than
  working for the nuns in the sixth grade and doing a

good job. I got the same kind of feedback and feeling of self-worth from the superior officers.

I got out of the navy shortly after John Kennedy said, "Ask not what your country can do for you . . . ," so I joined the CIA. I was asking what I could do for my country. The import of that lifestyle stayed with me till well past age thirty.

A turning point came during Larry's cursillo weekend. He found himself participating at an Anglican Eucharist. He was a Roman Catholic and knew the Church did not allow him to go to Communion. Yet, he felt drawn to share the sacrament. He looked around for the correct authority to tell him what to do, but for the first time in his life, authority eluded him.

That was a big conflict: a Catholic priest I knew well was seated behind me. The Anglican priest was in front of me. I was standing in the middle. I really had to examine who was making my decisions for me—a Catholic priest looking over my shoulder, God looking down at me, the Anglican priest at the altar, or me. At the time I think I opted for God and the Catholic priest, because I didn't go! But the event released a powerful process, a powerful force in me.

Whether or not I went to Anglican communion was not anywhere near as important as the fact that I realized that going to Anglican communion was my own choice to make. That was the result of the conflict. Going through that experience was so liberating and so exhilarating. I began to make decisions and feel good about them—political decisions, social decisions, a decision not to be a pilot for Pan Am, and a decision to make pottery. I was growing in confidence. I was learning to trust my own ability to make a decision.

Larry came to the realization that for years, a force inside himself had been controlling him. When that compelling force began to surface, Larry looked at it and found it wasn't really him. He began to listen to his *real* insides and to respond to his inner directives. The feeling that "they" always would know better than he was broken when he realized that the mysterious "they" were also tragically programmed people. When this happened, his feeling about *himself* changed drastically, too. He now can listen to himself and know that exhilarating feeling of being free and *right*. No uniform he wore had ever done this for him.

The cracks in Larry's secure world revealed that much of what he had relied upon was shaky, and he began more and more to find security within himself.

His wife and parents and some people who were important to him supported him in transition. "They gave me the feeling that I can do what I want and need to do, and now I feel that same way about myself."

RESPONSE

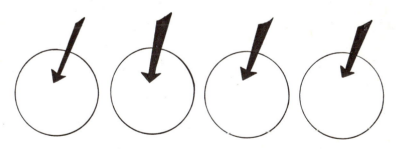

1. People   2. Authority   3. Beliefs   4. Identity

Each of the above circles represents a secure world which was discovered to have a crack in it. Write about some sources of security which are no longer part of your life—or at least are significantly changed.

1. *People* you once looked up to.

   _____

   _____

2. *Authority* which you once needed in order to act.

   _____

   _____

3. *Beliefs* or values you once held strongly.

   _____

   _____

4. An *identity*, a uniform, or a position that was really important to you.

   _____

   _____

Now choose one of the items you have recorded and describe in writing the experience of letting go. What were your feelings then? now? Write in some detail.

_____

_____

_____

_____

_____

_____

_____

_____

_____

Finally, summarize the *positive* aspects of the experience.

_____

_____

_____

_____

_____

Share as much as possible of this experience with the members of your group.

3 Cracks That Reappear

Most of us ignore cracks when they first appear in the security which encircles us. We swallow hard and hope they will go away. We even try to patch the cracks or paint them over so they will not be seen—most of all by ourselves!

But those cracks which signal life's transitions have a way of reappearing. When they do, the secure world we have tried to keep intact begins to close in around us.

Reappearing cracks and closed-in feelings are very much a part of Sara's story. When you meet Sara, she *expands*. Her round eyes fill with wonder, and she pours herself into new possibilities. At one point in her life Sara was trying to do a balancing act. She was a wife and mother. She was in graduate school. She was involved in a hospital ministry with cancer patients.

The cracks which appeared in Sara's secure world had been present since childhood. But in early adulthood, she had become "realistic" and plastered them over. Two pictures of herself as a child haunted Sara. The first was that

of a little girl in a parochial school uniform listening to the
sisters.

> I really bought the bit that everyone knew more than I
> did. I might have a good idea, but for all I knew it was
> a heresy. I couldn't be the one to judge that. I had a
> real rigid convent education for eight years. The result
> was that I really didn't trust myself. Before I would
> venture into anything, I would seek someone's ad-
> vice.

The second picture was that of a little girl listening to her
mother.

> My mother always gave me phrases of advice like
> "Nobody is single by choice. They're single because
> they just couldn't find somebody." My mother really
> believed that. In fact she definitely let her career go
> down the drain in order to be a wife and mother. She
> made me feel the same way. So I said, "No, I can't do
> both; I have to make a choice now."

So Sara swallowed her own desire for a career because
of her mother's advice. Sara had been married and had
five children when she realized that she couldn't live out
the choices she had been taught. She discovered *another*
child within herself, a child that never really fit into the
parochial school uniform and that could not accept its
mother's either-or. Discovering this child was a painful
awakening.

> One day we had gone out for dinner, all nine of us in
> the one car—baby, four boys, mother, dad, grandma
> and great grandma. (We never went anywhere with-
> out the whole contingent.) We were on the way
> home. I was jammed in the back of the car with the

five kids crawling all over me, while the other three
adults were up front. I realized right then that I had to
do something. I was going under. There wasn't much
left of me. I knew I had to get out.

Sara got out by taking some teacher-training and running
a preschool for a few years. Her work at the school
showed her the creative part of herself that had been sup-
pressed. "I realized that there was a creative, spontane-
ous, delightful, child-like part of myself that was just
screaming to break out. *I* was always putting myself
down."

Even though Sara's work in the preschool was a delight
for her, it was hard on her husband.

My work caused so many questions and problems
within my husband that after three years I bowed out.

I came back within the fold. The black sheep returned to the family. I was still struggling. I resented
his attitude and kept asking, "What does this mean
for our relationship if he can't handle it? What do I do
now?" I decided I wanted both of us to grow.

Sara described herself as "taking two steps forward and
one step back" for the sake of her marriage. She learned
slowly that it was all right for her to create tension and
then face the results of that tension. She returned to
school again. This time she got her Master's degree. Today
she is an associate in the pastoral care department of a
large hospital. Her principal duty is ministering to termi-
nally ill patients.

Sara is still doing a lot of *balancing* in her life. "One step
forward and two back." She had to get out of the house,
but she wanted to stay there, too. She felt she had to get
out of the hypocrisy she saw in the Church, but the
Church was home for her. She wanted to care for the
spiritual and emotional needs of others, but she was a

Catholic *woman*. She had to get out of being a "peace-at-all-costs, Latin-culture wife," but she loved her husband and did not want to be separated from him.

A great turning point for Sara was her discovery of *flexibility*. She learned to combine different patterns of movement without getting stuck in the new ones and without getting out of former patterns altogether.

She is a Catholic woman doing professional ministry with dying patients. She has a career. She is a wife. Although Sara would never say it has been easy, she is saying it is *possible* and she is saying it with her life.

For Sara, the recurring cracks in her secure world turned out to be openings into other worlds, where she has found room to live and move and grow.

RESPONSE

Perhaps you are receiving signals that you are suppressing something of yourself which you need to express. Some of these signals can be feelings of sickness, headaches, tensions, frustrations, or times of depressions.

The symbol below represents you and some of the "roads not taken." On the "pathways" jot down some of the directions in life you might have taken but did not. Some of these directions might be opportunities, relationships, career choices, interests, talents, or dreams.

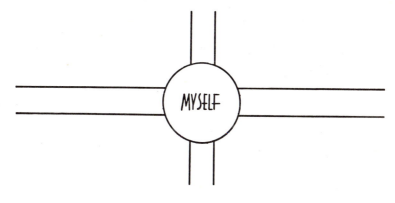

Now choose one of these paths and describe it in some detail.

_____

_____

_____

_____

_____

_____

_____

_____

_____

Can you, even in a small way, pursue this path now? How? (Note: Be creative in your answer. Most missed pursuits offer alternatives.)

_____

_____

_____

_____

If you are using this book in a group, share with the members of your group how you _feel_ about these reappearing cracks in your secure world. Listen carefully to what each person in the group is talking about. Try to hear the "music" behind the words.

4 *Shattered Worlds*

In most major life transitions, there is no way to move from the old and shattered world to a new and reintegrated world without passing through a period of painful adjustment. Life does not provide instant transitions. Facing and accepting transition sometimes means living in a shattered world for a long time.

Jane Louie is a women who has faced despair. Her story is a dramatic example of how a secure world can be shattered and can stay that way. It's hard to tell that now because Jane is so exuberant and outgoing, full of energy and humor.

Jane Louie grew up in San Francisco's Chinatown in the midst of the clang of cable cars and the lilt of Cantonese. She had been a drum majorette in high school and college. She marched to music, twirled her baton, and kept in step. Suddenly, the music stopped forever. While performing in Mexico City, she caught spinal meningitis and came out of the fever totally deaf.

Up until that time she had never even met a deaf person. "The first deaf person I ever met was in the mirror."

Jane's parents spoke only Cantonese, a language which relies on tones for meaning. Jane could not and cannot to this day read their lips. At age twenty-one she found herself alone in a silent world.

Before becoming deaf, I didn't need to stand up and speak for myself because I was one of the many. I was just as natural as you are. I could hear. I had no problem. I was one of the majority. I was free and alive. But all at once after the illness, I became one of the minority. That was the first real crisis I ever met.

When I became deaf, I said to myself, "What's this all about?" I'm not like everybody anymore. How do I act? Where do I turn? Who do I turn to? I asked all kinds of questions, but there were absolutely no answers. Nothing.

I said, "This just can't be *real*." I kept running and running. One day I stopped and looked at myself in the mirror. "I guess this is real. There's no use running anymore." But for a while I still ran. I ran as far as I could.

At home, I felt nothing but despair. All I did was weep. There was no way of comforting me. People said, "It's okay." How can anyone be so stupid as to say "It's okay" when they have no idea what it's all about?

Some people would say that they would pray for me. I would say to them, "Nothing doing." Their offer of prayers was like trying to feed me when I'm not hungry. It meant nothing.

Jane Louie had nowhere to go. She was no longer a hearing person. The people she had related to were cut out of her life. She could not understand them and they could not even begin to understand what she was going through. But she did not fit in with deaf people either. She had not grown up deaf. She had never learned sign language. The close-knit deaf community frightened her. Twenty-five years later, Jane is still dealing with the problem of not fitting in anywhere.

Hearing people don't believe that I am really deaf. That *hurts*, because I really don't hear anything. And deaf people will say, "You're lucky. You can speak."
I am in the middle, I don't really belong to either group. When you don't belong to any group, you feel *bad* about it. You are constantly fighting *inside yourself*. You keep telling yourself in little ways, "I really don't belong." I found myself on a see-saw. I kept going up and down.

For a long time Jane swallowed her pain. Then one day at work she surprised herself. She erupted, and all sorts of feelings poured out of her. A few people listened. She began to communicate a little bit more with them. She found herself talking to some hearing people.

Jane's new willingness to communicate was in no sense a solution. But in retrospect it proved to be the beginning of something. The next step came when she warily approached some deaf people. At first, she never let on she was deaf. But one day she attempted sign language. She discovered that she had the ability to use her hands effectively.

Gradually, Jane became more and more outgoing. In hearing groups, she made deaf people feel at home. In deaf groups she reached out to hearing people, included them, got them talking. Jane became a *link*. She found herself in between two groups of people who were *afraid* of each other, who couldn't *talk* to each other. And even though she felt clumsy, she could talk to both, she was part of both. Her problem became an opportunity.

It was as if she had been drowning in the bay between San Francisco and Oakland, without any hope of getting to either city. She then realized she could become a *bridge*. She could understand the hearing, and she could understand the deaf.

> I have a job to do. I have the job of bridging two worlds. Sometimes I feel I get stepped on, but I'm still glad people use the bridge. It's a pretty good feeling. Sometimes I get a little tired of it, but for the most part, I am proud of what I am.

In recent years, Jane has worked out a new way of relating to her deafness. She is still angry about it, but she is also grateful. She sees her deafness as a gift which brought her to a new world—a world where she never could have gone without it.

> For me, deafness is a real gift because it made me blossom. I probably would always have been a very sheltered homebody and never really gone out of the house more than I had to. But I had to come out of myself to understand my deafness. I came to understand myself a little better. I also came to a point where I could make decisions.
> My deafness was a kind of a second birth for me—a spiritual awakening. The person I was before died. I am no longer that person. And I had to accept that I am what I am *now*.

What Jane Louie lost never came back to her. Her hearing never came back. The meaning and relationships she had before did not come back either, but Jane moved into new meaning and new relationships. She discovered that the shattering of her world was somehow the key to her growth.

RESPONSE

The broken circle below is a symbol of shattered worlds—those experiences in the past that were unresolved. Within the circle write down any words which remind you of your own shattered worlds—unresolved experiences in your life which you still carry with you. Some of these might be relationships which ended badly, times when you were hurt or treated badly, illnesses, disappointments, or failures.

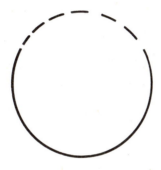

Now, pick one of the key words you have jotted down. Write about it in some detail. What was the experience like? How did it feel?

_____

_____

_____

_____

_____

_____

_____

_____

_____

_____

How do you feel about the unresolved area now?

_____

_____

_____

_____

_____

Share with the group whatever you feel free to share or choose to share about your shattered worlds.

PART TWO

Paths Emerging

There is another way, if you have the courage.
The first I could describe in familiar terms
Because you have seen it, as we have all seen it,
Illustrated, more or less, in lives of those about us.
The second is unknown, and so requires faith—
The kind of faith that issues from despair.
The destination cannot be described;
You will know very little until you get there;
You will journey blind. But the way leads towards
  possession of what you have sought for in the
  wrong place.

—T.S. ELIOT, The Cocktail Party

27

BEYOND CRISIS

The more we learn about crisis, the more we realize how difficult it is to really get beyond crisis. The choices we have are the choices we *see*. And the choices we see are limited. Crisis does not automatically open up new choices. But it can make us take a good hard look at the choices around us. If none of the choices really fit, then we're stuck. If we stay stuck, we keep living out choices which make us unhappy. Spiritual writers have often described the emergence of new paths in terms of darkness. The new choices we have to make are steps into darkness. Most of the time, even the shattered circle we leave behind looks more inviting than the shadows that lie ahead.

Choices that are different than the ones we have made lie beyond our familiar worlds. They are unknown and so require faith—the kind of faith which issues from despair. Our new journey is no longer on paths we know, but on paths which we are not even sure are there. Such a journey stretches through darkness and lets us know very little along the way.

But on the other side of the journey is a different world —a world which cannot be experienced by staying home or by looking back.

PREVIEW

Read the following statements. Then circle a number from 1-6 which shows how strongly you agree with each statement. (Very strongly—1, strongly—2, agree—3, agree somewhat—4, disagree somewhat—5, disagree strongly—6.

1. In general, people do not like to change.

     1   2   3   4   5   6

2. It is almost always better to work out your difficulties in your present situation than it is to try to change the situation.

   1   2   3   4   5   6

3. People who seek change are manifesting an inability to make a commitment.

   1   2   3   4   5   6

4. Someone who acts in unconventional ways is usually trying to attract attention to himself or herself.

   1   2   3   4   5   6

5. The pain of change is a warning signal that the change should not take place.

   1   2   3   4   5   6

6. Change and the pain of change are so important that it can be said that without them a person is not growing.

   1   2   3   4   5   6

7. A person who describes himself or herself as "in the dark" about something is usually showing a willingness to learn and grow.

   1   2   3   4   5   6

8. Even though a person's change may bring some distress to others, it is safe to say that those people would have experienced more distress if the change had not taken place.

   1   2   3   4   5   6

9. It is not really possible to accurately plot out a lifetime without budgeting in the possibility of change, darkness, and personal pain.

   1   2   3   4   5   6

10. **What a person does in life is never as important as how he or she feels about life.**

    1   2   3   4   5   6

    Circle which of the following axioms that best describes your attitude toward change.

    1. Blossom where you are planted.

    2. A rolling stone gathers no moss.

    3. When God closes a door, he opens a window.

Now, describe in some detail a time when you felt really in the dark about a personal decision.

_____

_____

_____

_____

_____

_____

_____

_____

Finally, discuss your answers in the group. Be prepared to explain your answers to the first two sections.

5 *Entering the Darkness*

In order to arrive at what you do not know
You must go by a way which is the way of ignorance.
In order to possess what you do not possess
You must go by the way of dispossession.
And what you do not know is the only thing you
    know.

—T.S. ELIOT, Four Quartets

In crisis, we enter the darkness of not knowing what to do about the future. Old paths end, but no new paths appear. We spend time wondering and worrying. Perhaps we try to escape the prospect of an unknown future. Some people try to cover their darkness with a mantle of bravado. Others throw themselves into work or pleasure. The lack of a sense of future feels a great deal like being dispossessed of comfortable and familiar furniture.

Will is an honest man. His curly hair is steely gray. His eyes are intense. The pain of growth and change is etched on his face. For a long time, he wrestled with being the associate rector of an affluent church and following out what he understood Christianity to be. The two realities did not square up for him.

> I found myself in radical conflict. I slowly realized that the Church was a culture, not a religion. And I didn't want to perpetuate a culture. I wanted to create a human experience.
>
> I couldn't stay there and maintain my integrity and my energy without killing myself. But I knew I couldn't just do my thing without seriously hurting some other people. When that all became evident, I had to leave. The move didn't happen easily or quickly. It happened over a terribly painful period of time.

After Will resigned, a group of influential parishioners asked him what he was going to do. When he told them that he honestly didn't know at that point, they accused him of the "sin" of confusion. They told him that he really needed straightening out. He came away from his meeting with the parishioners feeling bad about himself.

> I kept telling myself, "They're *right*. I *am* confused. I don't know what I'm going to do, and they all seem so certain of what they're doing."
>
> But deep inside, I knew they were wrong. Suddenly, it hit me. "Oh, they're right about one thing. I don't know what I am going to do. But they're wrong about something else. I'm not confused. I know damn well what I am *not* going to do anymore."

Will lived with that certainty during a time of difficult decisions. He *knew* what he was *not* going to do. Will managed not to jump at something he didn't really want just to get it all over with. He remained "in-between—for awhile, even though it was an uncomfortable place for him to be.

He didn't pretend he knew exactly where he was going, even though his honesty made a number of people who knew him shake their heads.

The greatest obstacle for anyone in learning something new is the need to pretend that he or she *already knows* what he or she needs to learn.

Will fumbled around a bit. He explored. He tried some things that didn't quite work. It is of the very nature of exploring not to know beforehand that which is being explored. If one knows beforehand, that person is not groping for anything *new*.

Eventually, Will found what he calls his "place for now." He and his family have 160 acres of farmland and are raising sheep. He has always loved the land, and he works hard. Will does marriage and family counseling two days a week. He also teaches and fills in at the local Anglican Church. The combination suits him.

When he looks back at the darkness, he sees it as a necessary part of his journey. Like the disillusionment which precedes enlightenment, like the dark night of John of the Cross, like the departure of Abraham for a place he did not know, darkness is a great teacher.

Only in the darkness do we learn to move step-by-step without having any master plan. Only in the darkness do we learn to keep going *without knowing*. Only in the darkness do we learn to trust our own instincts day-by-day. We learn the importance of taking steps which are not final solutions and which may not even seem to be leading to final solutions. If we wait for final solutions to become clear to us, we may never take any steps forward at all.

For some periods of our lives, it is necessary to proceed by the way of ignorance, where what we do *not* know is the only thing we really know.

RESPONSE

For a few moments, remember how you felt about the darkness when you were a child. Describe the feelings.

_____

_____

_____

_____

_____

Now recall a time when you were lost. Describe the feelings.

_____

_____

_____

_____

_____

On the chart below, write down three or four areas in your life which give you the feelings of darkness or of being lost. In the second column, try to sort out what you *do not* want to do or be anymore.

1. _____   _____

                                          _____

                                          _____

2. _____   _____

                                            _____

                                            _____

3. _____   _____

                                            _____

4. _____   _____

_____

_____

As an optional group experience, you may wish to share a trust walk. Each person in turn is blindfolded. While blindfolded, that person is led around the room by a "sighted" person. After each person has had a chance to both lead and be led, discuss the experience. In the context of this discus ere your answers to this section.

6 Living in Ambiguity

Many people face crisis in life and *make* decisions. But those who go furthest often do *not* make decisions immediately because they feel they can't. They cannot choose because the alternatives available to them all seem bad.

Crisis often presents us with a series of unacceptable choices, number of things we don't want to do. When there are no *good* choices available, the temptation is to settle for a bad one, and the reasoning runs along these lines: "I don't like any of my choices, but I have to do something; so I'll do this. What else can I do?"

Most traditional counseling tends to help people face their choices—to tell them they must make some decision. But almost everyone who has counseled people has noticed that some people wait. They refuse to choose because there does not seem to be any good choice available. Often the unexpected will happen.

People who refuse to settle for the "lesser of two evils" have to live with unacceptable choices. They go through a painful period where nothing makes sense. They live in a kind of ambiguity, sometimes for a period of years, without any apparent solutions. They keep grasping for straws, solutions which are not *there*.

It is precisely because people do *not* jump at immediate solutions that they slowly begin to grope their way out of that world of bad choices which oppresses them. It is by grappling with dead-ends that people change significantly. The grappling leads nowhere, but grappling long enough can free the struggle from the old ways of grappling.

In a powerful dream, Nikos Kazantzakis asked his grandfather for advice about how he should live his life. In the midst of rumblings of thunder and flashes of lightning his grandfather shouts, "Reach what you can!" But Nikos is not satisfied and cries out for a stronger reply. As the vision fades and the voice of his grandfather trails off into the distance, these words are left reverberating within him: "Reach what you cannot!" (*Report to Greco*).

Jack is a man who dealt with a lack of good choices. Jack looks like an anchorman from the evening news. He peers at you quizzically and talks with seriousness and sincerity. Sometimes it is hard to tell if he is kidding or not. He sees himself as a "do-gooder" and has always had lots of friends.

In his mid-forties, Jack made the decision to get out of public relations and management. "I spent a large part of my life lying for corporations, and I just didn't want to do that anymore." The decision to move was clear to him, but it was not clear to him where to go from there.

Jack had no real sense of what he wanted to do, except that he wanted to do something he believed in. He began fumbling around, looking, but not finding anything which offered a good salary! So he began doing something without a salary. He spent two years building up a nonprofit corporation which served the needs of deaf people. He sold one house and bought a less expensive one just to keep going. Along the way, he canceled his life-insurance policy because he decided he didn't need one anymore.

These were difficult years for Jack and his family—years of darkness and searching. His wife and several friends really supported him, but a number of people from his past felt he was mixed up. They were convinced that he simply could not get on with the task of living.

Through all this, Jack never lost the sense that he would find his place — that his convictions and talents would come together—but he did not know *how*. He persisted in refusing to do what he didn't believe in until he found and created a niche for himself. He is now using his corporate experience, and his writing and organizing abilities to help people live and act in a world of corporations. He is a social justice coordinator for the council of churches. In his position, he uses his corporate experience, often enough, to challenge large corporations themselves.

Jack recently finished producing a documentary on multinational corporations and the threat they pose to people and to human values. In characteristic fashion, he threw a large party at the Press Club to show the movie to corporate people!

Jack still has some bad feelings about the period of confusion in his life. He still feels that perhaps he was unfair to his family or was being too idealistic. But he is delighted about what he became because of that. He acts and decides with a great strength now. Fear is gone from him. His values are different. During his period of transition, deep changes took place in *him*.

> I really believe that if I don't free myself, I'm not going to help anyone. It's easy for me to think I'm helping someone else without making changes in myself. What has been very strong in me the past few years is the realization that the important thing is what *I* do, and not so much what I get other people to do.

Jack is nearing sixty now and is searching out next steps. He is looking for something less demanding and hectic for the next period of his life. "I guess I am facing the new all over again. But this time, I am not so frightened—not like last time." He knows now where the new will come from.

What Jack was reaching for did not appear until he was ready for it. But he kept reaching without seeing. Many people attempt to reach what they cannot. The reality they know becomes intolerable for them and they have to get beyond it or be crushed by it. So they fight reality. They slowly let go of their lives as they have lived them, and move beyond where they have been into the unknown.

No new world of choices appears before them full-blown, but little steps do appear, steps which seem inconsequential at the time. What is important is that they take such steps even though they do not seem to be leading anywhere. For such steps often lead to new alternatives which were previously out of reach and beyond imagining. If people jump at a final solution prematurely, their choices are limited to the best of a bad lot. It is only by taking the little *steps* available to them (steps which do not seem to lead to solutions) that they get out of the world of bad choices. For to get out of that world, they need to reach a different level. There is almost a rule about such profound change: No problem can be satisfactorily resolved at the same level which led to the problem in the first place.

RESPONSE

Describe a time or an area in your life in which you had no really good choices. This should be some situation in which you had to choose solutions which were all undesirable. What did you do? (Note: This need not be something earth-shattering.)

_____

_____

_____

_____

_____

_____

If there is any area in your life right now in which you would like to do something but see no clear options, briefly describe it here.

_____

_____

_____

_____

_____

The graphic below represents the journey into darkness. Reflect on the situation you have just described. Stop looking for an ultimate solution. Instead, on the lines below, write key words which signify little steps you can take or things you can explore that are not solutions but are steps.

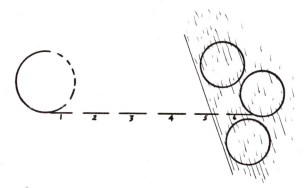

Share with the group the meaning of the key words. Then, try taking some of the little steps. Try not to have any great expectations.

7 _Grappling with Dilemma_

Sometimes the alternatives we know become impossible. Crisis can take the form of a dilemma or a double bind. A double bind is a set of circumstances in which you are "damned if you do and damned if you don't." A classic double bind is the humorous portrayal of the mother who buys two shirts for her son. Her son puts on one of the shirts. The mother immediately wails: "I just knew you wouldn't like the other one."

In his book, _Steps to an Ecology of Mind,_ Gregory Bateson describes an experiment with a female dolphin which indicates what can happen when someone is faced with seemingly impossible choices. The point of the experiment was to get the dolphin to invent new kinds of behavior.

The dolphin's trainer changed the signals the dolphin knew in order to purposely frustrate her. When she did what she was supposed to do, she would _not_ get a reward. (What used to work for her no longer worked.) Instead, she was given a fish only if she came up with new behavior—behavior which heretofore had not been rewarded. The dolphin was intentionally confused. She was consistently put into situations in which she did not know what to do. In these situations, her accustomed behavior brought no rewards.

During the experiment, the dolphin went through agony. Her relationship with the trainer was severely strained. Occasionally, the trainer went back to the old rules and gave the dolphin a reward even when she did not deserve it. The occasional rewards were meant to keep the dolphin interested.

For fourteen sessions, the animal kept doing the same things she had always done and kept repeating behavior which had been rewarded in the past. The experiment seemed to be getting nowhere.

But in the time out between the fourteenth and fifteenth sessions, the porpoise appeared to be much excited, and when she came onstage for the fifteenth session, she put on an elaborate performance including eight conspicuous pieces of behavior of which four were entirely new—never before observed in this species of animal.

Bateson draws two conclusions:

First, that severe pain and maladjustment can be induced by putting a mammal in the wrong regarding its rules for making sense of an important relationship with another mammal. Second, that if pathology can be warded off or resisted, the total experience may promote creativity.

The dolphin was being forced to let go of ways of acting which had worked in the past—ways of relating which had always brought rewards. She was being forced to let go of the only ways she knew. The pressure on her was extreme, and there was concern that it would drive her crazy.

What kept her going was her relationship with the trainer. She needed someone on her side—someone who could understand the pain she was going through and who would care. She needed someone who would not leave her alone and who would provide some stability in a very disturbing situation. Perhaps most important, she needed someone who would encourage her to keep going — someone who believed she was getting somewhere even though she felt she was getting nowhere.

In crisis, each of us is pressed to let go of ways we have known. Like the dolphin, we do not understand what is happening to us at the time. We are not in control and cannot get back into control. We simply have to live through the experience.

The important question is not "What am I going to do?" The important question is "Who will be there for me?" We need to communicate about our pain and our fear. We need to let go and become vulnerable. We need to trust someone in ways we may never have trusted before. Ultimately, we need someone who will not try to solve our problems for us. We need someone who will keep us moving and see us through the pain to a new place—a place we cannot see but only weakly believe is there.

In his forties, Ben came face to face with intolerable alternatives. He entered deeply into dilemma. "I knew that my drinking was killing me, but I simply could not face life sober."

Ever since he was a child, Ben had been searching. He didn't have much trust in his parents. He was very bright and could see through a lot of things that happened in his life. He feels that his grandfather understood him and ultimately saved his spirit.

Ben's search brought him into the intellectual world— the world of poetry and the arts. The search also led him into the labor movements, where he tried to organize workers and fight the structure of giant corporations. But his search also landed him in a deep dependency on alcohol. It was years before Ben acknowledged his alcoholism and sought the support and the help of Alcoholics Anonymous.

I've grown to know in a crude kind of way what grace is supposed to be. I have been willing to say that it was a gift I certainly did not earn. I didn't have the means within myself to stop drinking. Yet, I wanted some kind of peace and sanity. That gift was given me by a group of men who loved me. They simply would not let me down. It took me a long time to realize what these people were helping me do.

Ben did not see a way out of his disease. Breaking out of the dilemma did not entail figuring out what to do about the problem; rather, it meant a deep change in him. Ben did not change the dilemma. The dilemma changed him. He began to let new realities and feelings and relationships break into his life.

I don't know what keeps me going. I just think I'm damn lucky. I could say that it was faith, hope, and love, but those things seem like just blown-up words. What I do know is that I'm being nourished. I have never trusted people. I have been afraid to. But people have trusted me. My grandfather told me long ago that I would be a somebody. But it is only today that I am beginning to understand what he meant. It's funny, but I think I wouldn't have been any damn good if I hadn't been a drunk!

Today, Ben senses possibility all around him—even in dire situations. He has passed through some dead-ends in his lifetime. He has also experienced the joyful surprise when at the very end of the road a beautiful pathway opens.

I regard myself as having been reborn more than once in my lifetime. That rebirth came through people who cared—even when I didn't notice. I had to stop looking before I found the support I needed. What a surprise! And what promise!

RESPONSE

You have no doubt experienced dilemmas in your lifetime—times when you were "damned if you did and damned if you didn't." In the first column below, briefly describe three such dilemmas. In the second column, list some of the "no-win" alternatives.

Dilemma	Alternatives
1. _____	_____
	_____
	_____
2. _____	_____
	_____
	_____
3. _____	_____
	_____
	_____

Now select one of the above dilemmas and describe in some detail what you chose to do about it.

_____

_____

_____

_____

_____

_____

Now briefly describe how you *felt* about the outcome.

_____

_____

_____

_____

Be prepared to share these feelings with the group. When sharing these feelings, be sure to look for clues as to how each of the alternatives felt. Look, too, for clues to alternatives that may not have been as evident.

Another possibility would be to act out without words (pantomime) how you felt when you were faced with a dilemma. Act out, too, the attempts you made to resolve your situation.

PART THREE

New Ways

There is a critical point in the development of a person, when a person realizes that his decisions affect him more deeply than they affect events outside himself. The critical point occurs when a person finds out for himself that it's up to him to decide what he is to make of himself.

—BERNARD LONERGAN, Collection

People who face crisis often begin the process of resolution by trying to find answers outside themselves. They look for books, classes, friends, groups, or some other outside force that will take away the agony of their personal struggle. But some people reach a point at which their struggle begins to change *them*.

Once this point is reached, the emphasis shifts from changing my situation to changing *me*. The journey then consists not so much in figuring out alternatives as it does in becoming a new person. From this newness will emerge the new ways — ways which will resolve the dilemma.

The principal element of this change is the ability to let go. The old way of facing life is very compelling because it is familiar (even if it is painful). But when the crisis undermines the hold of the former way of dealing with life, the new ways do emerge—new ways of seeing, deciding, and relating.

PREVIEW

Read the following paragraph. When you have finished the reading, answer the questions as honestly as you can.

Barbara's husband had been dead for five years. She had made no attempts to remarry or to change the patterns of life that she had established when her husband was alive. She had two grown children and five grandchildren. She loved her children, but somehow their attentions could not break through an increasing feeling of dread and loss. Barbara was in her mid-sixties, but she began to seem much older. Everything was a chore. She missed her husband more than she did at the time of his death. Nothing could penetrate the shroud of gloom that had settled around her. Her religious faith, which she practiced with ever-increasing vigor, seemed to help not at all. She tried some psychiatric therapy, but dropped it after only a few sessions. Her friends and family grew more and more concerned. Their advice and scolding was received and accepted, but to no avail. The crisis in Barbara had grown to the point of despondency.

1. In two or three words, what do you feel is Barbara's problem.

_____

2. What are three or four logical alternatives which you would suggest to help relieve Barbara's depression?

_____

_____

_____

_____

3. Can you describe a crisis in your own life which left you with many logical "outs" none of which you could bring yourself to follow?

_____

_____

_____

_____

_____

4. How do you react to Barbara's crisis? How does her problem make you feel?

_____

_____

_____

5. What changes can take place in Barbara which would help her break out of her crisis?

_____

_____

_____

_____

—————————————————————————

—————————————————————————

Discuss with the group the answers that have been given to these questions. Discuss, too, the meaning of the sentence, "Some people reach a point at which their struggle begins to change them."

8 *Seeing Differently*

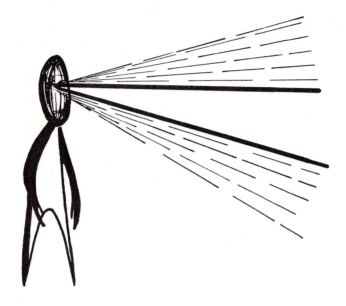

Crisis is often an eye-opener—a time when people let go of former ways of viewing reality and begin to see differently. There is nothing more unreachable than a blind person who insists that he or she can see. The admission of blindness is often the first step toward a new perception.

Ed had to face a slow process of disillusionment with his company and a reexamination of the way he looked at life. That was only part of Ed's crisis experience.

> During the first ten years of our marriage, I was totally dedicated to climbing the corporate ladder. Each step up demanded more of me. I was courting high blood pressure and a ruined marriage. Finally, Mary and I came to a decision. I had to slow down. I could not afford to lose any more of myself. So my goals began to change and differ from the company's. We decided that money and advancement weren't that important. I thought I could maintain a level in the corporation without fighting for the next rung.

That was harder than I thought. I saw people passing me. I knew I was better. The old football mentality
kept creeping in—the drive to win. But I also began to
realize that the company really wanted just a bigger
and bigger slice of me. I was not making decisions—
the corporation was. I had liked the thrill of the chase.
Devising marketing plans and making quotas was
fun. But when the day was through, I had no idea
what I had truly accomplished. That was the source of
my frustration.

Once Mary and I decided to short circuit all that, we
began to feel free. I was no longer living to please the
guy I was working for. I began to make decisions in
order to make me feel good without undue regard for
the consequences. I was not advancing, and yet I felt
more productive than I had in years. It was like I had
been working blind.

The shattering of illusions is painful, but it is an important step in learning. We begin to learn only after we
realize that what we thought we knew all along was mis-
taken. "It is because you insist that you can see that your
blindness persists" (*John* 9:41). We have to let go of our
former ways of seeing. Our problem usually is not blindness. It is thinking that we can see.

Father Karl went to the Philippines as a missionary. He
went thinking he could see.

I went to the Philippines with my shoes on, an Ameri-
can flag in one hand and a papal flag in the other.

After some years there, he lost his shoes and his flags.
He described himself as a barefoot padre holding hands
with his people under the coconut trees. In 1973 he was
asked to leave the country by the Marcos government.

Karl describes his first years working with the Catholics
in the parishes—especially the leaders.

I sided with the wealthy, the educated, and the powerful. Why wouldn't I? I came from an upper middle class family in Iowa. I always walked purposefully with my head held high. I played to the hilt the role of the good priest in the white cassock. I defended my position as one of the "betters" because I never really questioned myself.

The beginning of change came when Karl noticed that some things did not fit. Everywhere there were the barefoot people, the fishermen, the poor who didn't come to church. He tried to work with the rich to change the social system until he realized that the people who did not fit were the key to his mission in the Philippines. These were not the rich but the people across the river — the barefoot people who ate with their fingers, who could not own land or even borrow money.

One day Karl stopped being blind. "It dawned on me—I am on the wrong side of the river." Karl had been spending his time on the side of the river where the church *building* was, but the people who were the Church—who needed and appreciated the good news — were on the other side. Like a blind man drunk with the gift of sight, Karl crossed the river and began spending his time with the poor.

There Karl was exposed to the depth of oppression. He opened himself to that oppression and became one of the poor. In this way he left the old choices—the circles he had grown up in. He left for the first time the context of middle class America and the context of the "normal" Catholic. He looks back at the way he was before with some amusement.

I am so different now. I don't know what would have become of me if I had not gone to the Philippines or if I had not crossed the river. I suppose I would be the same as I was with the same upper middle class values my family and friends have.

Karl let his life change by letting in people and events which at first threatened him. These people and events changed both his view of the world and his view of himself. He let go of former ways of seeing, or better, he added a new way of seeing.

Most of us adults develop filters. We screen out events which threaten us—new relationships, new ways of doing things, new ways of acting, etc. We make perceptual decisions and see only what we want to see. We see only what we can tolerate. Such blindness limits our ability to imagine alternatives for ourselves. Such blindness makes our world smaller and begins to stunt our growth.

Personal enlightenment is nothing very mystical. We do not have to wear saffron robes or sit cross-legged on the floor chanting mantras. What we do need for personal enlightenment is to get beyond the junk and nonsense in our lives to what is really there. Pretending is a prison. Seeing reality is the key that sets us free.

One concept that is very important in Christianity is the process called *metanoia* — deep change of mind and heart and attitude. For almost everyone, deep changes of heart begin with the admission of blindness. Those who enter into a process of change carry with them the awareness that their view is always partial—open to revision, change, and surprise. Such people remain open to the new. They never fool themselves into thinking that they see everything clearly again.

Insisting that we can see can lead to permanent blindness. Admitting our blindness can lead to a new and constantly expanding vision.

RESPONSE

Each of us looks at our world from a unique perspective. Each of us has a horizon beyond which we do not see. Our horizon is the boundary of our vision. Because we see everything on this side of the horizon, we often have diffi-

culty seeing or discovering anything beyond it. As someone once said, "I don't know who discovered water, but I
know it was not a fish."

One of the most helpful steps a human being can take is to
begin to realize his or her limited vision—or horizon. This step
is a discovery of what one does not know. In the first of the two
boxes below, list some situations in your life about which you
have a fixed horizon—a definite stand or opinion. These could
be situations or events that do not fit for you—that bother you.
They should be things that are somehow asking you to expand
your horizons.

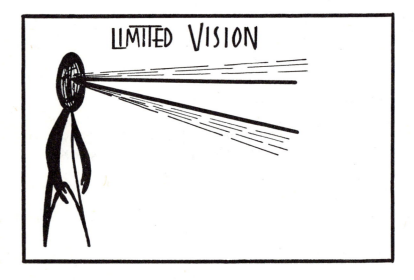

Now in the next box, describe in some detail an experience in
which you had your horizon expanded so that you got a broader
perspective.

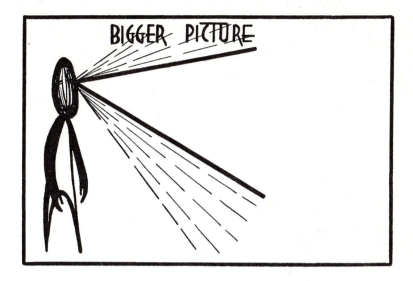

Now, pick one of the bothersome situations from the first box and describe how you think this situation could help you to expand your horizon.

_____

_____

_____

_____

_____

In your group, discuss how the prospects of admitting blindness makes you feel. Do not be satisfied with superficial answers like "frightened" or "anxious." Probe for more specific answers. Listen for the clues that you and other members of the group may be dropping.

9 Deciding Differently – Drawing in Your Own Box

Many people drift through life doing, thinking, and saying what they were taught or what they hear others in their own circle are doing, thinking, or saying. When faced with a choice or when given a vision that is different, many people succeed in missing the meaning of the experience. They return to the human condition as T.S. Eliot describes it.

> (They) maintain themselves by the common routine,
> learn to avoid excessive expectation,
> Become tolerant of themselves and others,
> Giving and taking, in the usual actions
> What there is to give and take. They do not repine;
> Are contented with the morning that separates
> And with the evening that brings together
> For casual talk before the fire
> Two people who know they do not understand each
>   other,
> Breeding children whom they do not understand
> And who will never understand them.
>
> —*The Cocktail Party*

To begin to decide differently—to meet crisis head on—
is a work of imagination and courage. It demands creating
a way that is different from the way that is provided by
convention.

Creativeness means imagining something different,
something better and higher. Imagination calls up before us something better than the reality around us.
Creativeness always rises above reality.

—NICHOLAS BERDYAEV, *The Destiny of Man*

Once, when I was moving out of town, a friend sold my
car for me, but he neglected to send the change-of-
ownership forms to the state capital. The Department of
Motor Vehicles was quite unaware that I no longer owned
the car. The new owner proceeded to pile up a number of
parking tickets. I began to get the bills for them.

I wrote a most pleasant letter to the police explaining
that I no longer owned the car. I received my own letter
back in the mail. Stamped in red was the notice, "Please
Remit!" I wrote again to explain that there must be some
mistake. Since I did not hear anything for three months, I
supposed that the matter was settled.

Then, I received a letter stating that a warrant was being
issued for my arrest if I did not pay the fines immediately.
I can still see the letter. It was a printed form. There were
two boxes at the bottom. "Check one" said the terse in-
structions. The first box was labeled, "Enclosed is my
payment." The second box was labeled with the equivalent of "Come and get me." Phone calls to the police got
me a recorded message which told me, "Warrants is busy.
Please call later."

I was stuck. The more I stared at those two boxes, the
worse I felt. What could I do? I began to feel that I had
better send the money. What else was there to do? I felt
helpless, frustrated, and depressed. But then another feeling began to replace the others—anger. "I will not send

them that money and I will not check either of their stupid boxes."

I grabbed a black pen and directly under the other two boxes I traced another box just like them. Next to the new box I printed the words, "Letter to Chief of Police Enclosed." I checked the box and wrote the letter. In a matter of days, I received a letter of apology and I did not have to pay the fines.

I had gone beyond the alternatives that had been given to me, and the success gave me great feeling of satisfaction.

In moments of personal crisis we spend a lot of time staring at our alternatives. We find ourselves staring at the possible boxes. The more we mull over the choices that are apparent, the more hopeless our situation seems. It is only when we reject the apparent choices that we can begin to struggle to draw in our own boxes — to assert our own power to imagine and to decide.

Phillip spent a good part of his life grappling with choices which didn't fit him. He was always trying to be someone he could not be. Today there is a small restaurant on Monterey Bay in California that is run by a bearded man with twinkling eyes who will welcome you and serve you with obvious delight and personal pleasure. The man is Phillip. The atmosphere in the restaurant is warm and friendly. Some of Phillip's weavings hang on the walls. You might even convince Phillip to sing one of the songs he has written.

If on the following Sunday you were to attend a large Roman Catholic Church in the suburbs, you might recognize the celebrant of the Mass as the same man who sang and served in the restaurant. You might hear him preaching with the same warmth and good humor you experienced in the small bayside restaurant.

It took Phillip years to discover a world of choices in which he was not controlled by people and circumstances.

The whole journey began because Phillip felt that he did not fit into the collar and cassock.

In the seminary and later in the priesthood, I always felt that I was in the wrong place. But I still wanted very much to be where I was. In fact, I never wanted to be anywhere else. That confused me. I was always dealing with tension. I somehow felt like I was always faking it—trying to do something I shouldn't do.

In my parish work, I felt that I was doing very little well. Oh, I celebrated Mass well and I knew that I was effective in the confessional. As I look back now, I guess I did a lot of good, but I was very unsure of myself because the good I was doing was not done the way it was *supposed* to be done. I was always feeling guilty. I began to question the Church. Then I questioned society and the kinds of conventions that made me feel so out of place. And, of course, I questioned myself.

Well, to fight those questions I began to do an immense amount of "people" things. I started youth groups and worked with all the parish organizations. I gave retreats and spent extra time counseling people. All the while, I knew it wasn't going to work.

The turning point came when Phillip stopped questioning himself and began questioning again the Church and society's conventions. He began to ask who in fact was out of line? Who didn't fit? Maybe he was being asked to fulfill a role that had very little to do with Christianity.

Phillip began to let go of the images he had been trying to live up to. He got hurt, and he experienced failure. He fell in love with someone who could let him feel vulnerable and could let him show weakness. He began to accept himself as he was, without having to pretend anymore.

With the priesthood as it was, Phillip did not fit in. He faced the usual choices men make when they do not fit into the priestly mold — pretending or leaving. Phillip could do neither. He hated pretending, and he did not want to leave. So he began to do something that made sense to him. He began to create his own choices and began to feel good about them. The restaurant business felt right, and his ministry in the parish felt right. So he began putting the two together in a very unlikely combination.

Today, Phillip is living a full and happy life. Some people have difficulty with his living in more than one context. Phillip now recognizes their reactions are their problem, not his. His life makes sense to him. After having dealt with impossible choices, he faced the challenge of making his own life make sense and his own story work —a challenge he is enjoying and is carrying on.

> I make a lot of little decisions. Somehow or other what I am doing is working out—as long as I keep myself open to possibilities. It is up to me to decide what I am going to make of myself. I just cannot be static.

In any decision what has been achieved is always precarious. It can slip, fall, shatter. But what is to be achieved in the future can be ever-expanding and deepening. Every challenge which is met reveals another challenge.

Once we reach this point in a crisis, we are no longer controlled either by inner compulsions or by the need to conform to what others expect of us. We are beyond the categories of behaving and misbehaving. We have become capable of creative activity — creating our own stories by developing a sense of what is right and following through on that sense. We stop looking outside ourselves for the judgment of our actions. We look instead to the "inner court" where the self becomes its own plaintiff, judge, and jury.

We can then stop living in fear of making mistakes because we sense that we will be able to correct what is wrong in time. We then become capable of growth—self-corrective change. The former security of a settled future vanishes and a new security comes from responding to events rather than from trying to control the future in advance.

It is in creating new boxes that the child-like freedom to try new things returns. We learn again the ability to risk, to be clumsy and not *have* to succeed. Perhaps this is what is meant by becoming "like little children"—an openness to wonder, discovery, and simple trust.

RESPONSE

In each of the boxes below, describe a situation in which you do not feel comfortable. These could be boxes you experience at home, boxes at work, boxes that other people put you into.

☐ ☐ ☐ ☐ ☐

Now pick one of the situations and in the first column below list some of the possible solutions you are given by society, family, superiors, or the like. In the second column, try to create a "new box." Describe a creative response to the situation.

Conventional Boxes   **The New Box**

In the group, discuss some of the situations that have been described and begin to expand on the possibilities. Brainstorm as many creative "new boxes" as possible for each situation. There are no rules for thinking up possibilities. (Write some of these possibilities on the diagram below.)

10 *Relating Responsibly*

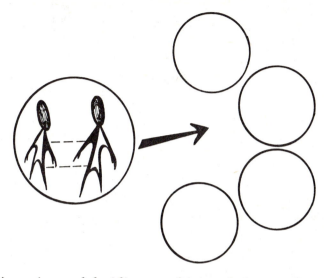

As in seeing and deciding, so also in relating, we live with patterns from our past—fixations and habits we may not even be aware of. It is only when we begin to feel discomfort or pain or loss in a relationship that we get the opportunity to really examine the way we relate to others. Then we can see what we have been doing with someone else, and we can see what that other person has been doing to us. Often we can continue to act our our part of a relationship without ever questioning the other half. We act as though we are unaware that the context of the relationship —the interaction of two people—is really the heart of that relationship.

There was a pastor in New York City who rose to some political prominence as an advocate for the poor. Whenever he entertained another political person, he would seat him or her, pour a drink, raise his glass and proclaim, "All right. How can you use me and how can I use you?"

By that proclamation the pastor brought into the open the unspoken context of a political relationship. He wanted to be clear about what he was doing with someone and what that person was doing with him. Only when we realize what is going on in a relationship can we *see* that we have choices. Only when the context is visible can what is wrong in a relationship be adjusted or corrected.

Many people are like Mary. She spent years of her life counseling others. She was not really a professional counselor. In fact, other than a few years in the convent, she had no human relations training at all. But she gradually built up a reputation among friends and neighbors. She was recognized as a kind of "earth-mother" who would listen to all tales of woe and would dispense advice free of charge. Mary really needed that feeling of having people depend on her.

Soon Mary began to resent the drain on her time and energy. She started hating those same friends and neighbors that had been for so long a source of her own identity in her community. Mary began to have symptoms of anxiety and panic. She no longer was comfortable in her relationships. Her husband was alarmed at the change in her. But her resentment was largely misplaced. Soon she began to realize that the source of her crisis was not the flock of dependent people in her life. She had been acting out her end of the pattern. She was sending out vibrations which clearly said, "I like to help. I like having people depend on me."

When people did depend on Mary, she got angry at them. She was in a trap partly of her own making. When it became intolerable, Mary had to learn to let go of her need to be a helper and a counselor and had to allow herself to be vulnerable and to be helped. Mary sought professional help herself. While her former "clients" were somewhat dumbfounded, Mary herself began to grow creatively in her relationships to others by changing the context that she had set up.

When former ways of relating no longer work for us, we can experience a lot of pain, but we also can become capable of learning new ways of relating. Consuela is a woman who felt the pain of letting go in a relationship. She went through agony when her daughter decided to leave home. Once her daughter was gone, Consuela realized that what she thought had been love for her daughter was really her need for her daughter to be something for *her*—something to fulfill her dreams and designs.

> You can control people to some extent. But there is a danger in trying. We should be, I suppose, able to control ourselves, but our control of others is at best an illusion. When my daughter left home, I was desperate because I never thought she would do it. I was sure that I had the power and control to prevent her leaving. I was her mother. I had the say. But the shock was that I really had no say at all. Now I know that I never want to love anyone that way. Not even my own family. People cannot belong to me. There is freedom in loving somebody enough to say, "God bless you. Go your way."

Consuela learned to recognize the context of her relationship with her daughter. She grew through the pain of loss, but she did grow.

Shirley was on the other end of a controlling relationship. She learned to recognize her end of a pattern that she had established with her husband and do something to change it.

> What has changed in me? Well, whenever anything needed to be done in my life, my husband would tell me how to do it, and I did it. I scarcely had a single thought of my own in my head. It's not that my husband is a tyrant or anything. It's just that I had created a role for myself in which I did not have a single thought or desire of my own.

I couldn't understand why I always felt so angry. I didn't know how to handle anger. I couldn't handle confrontations without giving in. I would sell my soul for peace. But for all my attempts, I felt no peace. I was convinced that I could not do battle with my husband verbally. He could annihilate me on that level. But for the most part that was not true. And the biggest change is that those verbal annihilations just do not happen anymore.

The games I used to play with myself were really quite humorous. If something happened during the day I thought would be at all disturbing to my husband, I would tell the boys, "Please, don't tell your dad what happened." I had a whole system of tricks to keep him from seeing what I considered to be my stupidity.

I ended up in therapy. You see, my husband did not like the role he was cast in. But he used my expectations to get me some professional help. Well, I began to see that I was really responding not to my husband but to patterns that went back to my relationship to my parents. That was like a big light going on. I could pull back and look at my relationships. After seeing what had been happening, I started to change. I began to change how I reacted to people and how I expected them to react to me. I knew the change was stabilizing when my husband said to me, "You know, it doesn't do me any good to get angry around here anymore." Unconsciously, my husband was using anger to control me. When my expectations changed so did his and we began again to grow together.

The most basic sign of growth in relationships is the realization that a person does not need to be one way *or* the other in a relationship. A person can be strong and weak, dominant and submissive. This is a sign of a developing *response-ability*. Such a realization shows that a person is able to choose responses in relationships. Most mammals can be trained to respond the same way in similar situations. It is the sign of human activity to be able to vary responses.

There is a difference between reliability and responsibility. The reliable person acts predictably. He or she pays bills on time or returns phone calls. The responsible person discerns and chooses. Keeping things the same all the time in a relationship just does not work. In fact, such an attempt can undermine a relationship. We all fear such change and loss. But our demand for permanence or stability in a relationship may mean that we do not want the relationship to grow and be nourishing. Rather we may want someone to cling to or someone clinging to us. A relationship based on clinging, if it remains that way, can only be harmful.

It is important to emphasize that letting go of fixed patterns of relating does not mean putting an end to a relationship. But it may mean facing the other person with a choice. It usually means allowing the other person the opportunity to be himself or herself — to make his or her own decisions.

Anais Nin describes letting go in terms of the dance of "the woman without arms."

My arms were taken away from me, she sang.
I was punished for clinging.
I clung. I clutched all those I loved;
I clutched at the lovely moments of life;
    my hands closed upon every full hour.
My arms were always tight craving to embrace.
I wanted to embrace and hold
    the light, the wind, the sun, the night
    and the whole world.
I wanted to caress, to heal, to rock, to lull,
    to surround, to encompass.

And I strained and held so much that they broke;
They broke away from me.
Everything eluded me then. I was condemned not to
    hold.
Trembling and shaking she stood looking at her arms
    now stretched before her again.
She looked at her hands tightly closed
And opened them slowly, opened them completely
    like Christ;
She opened them in a gesture of abandon and giving;
She relinquished and forgave, opening her arms and
    her hands,
Permitting all things to flow away and beyond her.
And she danced; she danced with the music
    and with the rhythm of earth's circles;
And turned with the earth's turning, like a disc,
Turning all faces to light and to darkness evenly,
    dancing toward daylight.

—*House of Incest*

RESPONSE

In the first column below list three relationships you have had in
the past. Then in the second column describe some changes you
had to go through in these relationships.

     Relationships   **Changes**

1. _____   _____

                                 _____

                                 _____

2. _____   _____

                                 _____

                                 _____

3. _____   _____

_____

_____

Can you describe any patterns that are common to these relationships?

_____

_____

_____

_____

Now describe your two most important relationships now. What
patterns seem to predominate in these relationships. What
choices do you make or neglect to make in responding to the
person to whom you are relating?

Relationship One:

_____

_____

_____

_____

_____

Relationship Two:

_____

_____

_____

_____

_____

Use the following diagram to describe briefly one of the two relationships you have just written about. Try to find four symbolic words which best describe the relationship.

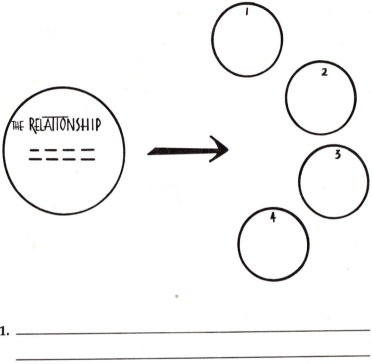

1. _____

_____

2. _____

_____

3. _____

_____

4. _____

_____

Then answer the following questions about the relationship.

1. What have I been doing in the relationship?

    _____

    _____

2. Why have I been doing that?

    _____

    _____

3. What would I like to do in the relationship?

    _____

    _____

4. How am I going to change?

    _____

    _____

In the group, discuss your answers to the four questions. Be aware of different ways people have of expressing their desire for change.

PART FOUR

Creating a New Story

Those not busy being born are busy dying.

—BOB DYLAN

After my grandmother died, everyone was sitting in the funeral home silent and solemn when great-aunt Kluber appeared. Kluber was ninety at the time. She walked briskly to the front, greeting people along the way. She knelt for a moment by the casket. She rose, crossed herself, and took a seat, ram-rod straight near the front. Her eyes darted all about the room and finally settled again on the casket. In the silence of the chapel, Kluber's stage whisper was almost a shout, "Joe Bacigalupi used to make them boxes for thirty-five dollars. Look at the price they're getting for them now!"

Some people were shocked. Others pretended they did not hear. Most people considered her an eccentric. But great-aunt Kluber had just taken a good look at life and decided not to fit into the prevalent insanity. The context did not make sense to her anymore. So, she did not pretend that it did. She was not one whit shy about letting people know about her discovery.

Kluber was a great character. She was a woman who moved beyond the context surrounding her and created a story that truly was her own.

People who begin to move out of contexts into which they no longer fit feel bad about themselves at first. It is only after a new life comes together for them that they can look back and see what they have left behind. If they keep "busy being born," other contexts open up and they begin living in more than one context. Soon moving into new contexts becomes a way of life.

Most of us can best see contexts after we are out of them. School, the service, a destructive relationship, or different periods of our lives, once passed through, give us summaries of the choices and mistakes we have made. How often have we almost sighed, "If I only knew then what I know now." In the previous section of this book, you explored new ways in terms of changing contexts of seeing, deciding, and relating. In this section, you will be looking at the potential these new ways have for re-creating you — for helping you write your own story.

Hopefully, you can look back and appreciate former contexts for what they were. You can experience a certain freedom. You need no longer feel judged by past circles or feel the need to justify yourself for moving on. The past stages of the journey are simply necessary steps along the way.

The real opportunity of walking the paths through crisis is to integrate experiences from the past, relish and embrace the unfolding present, and from a rich variety of experiences, put the unlikely together for your future.

PREVIEW

Read each of the following five statements. After each, circle the word which best describes your reaction.

1. **Today is the first day of the rest of your life.**
   a. hokey
   b. profound
   c. misleading
   d. significant
   e. ridiculous

2. **The purpose of rules and regulations is to share the wisdom of experience with those who might lack either wisdom or experience.**
   a. patronizing
   b. true
   c. realistic
   d. frightening
   e. prophetic

3. **To thine own self be true and it must follow as the night the day, thou canst not then be false to any man.**
   a. accurate
   b. overstressed
   c. undisciplined

d. essential
e. unfounded

4. **For a relationship to be stable, it must embrace as part of its very existence the concept of change and growth.**
   a. hum-bug
   b. revolutionary
   c. perfect
   d. undermining
   e. promiscuous

5. **Faith supplies the challenge and the driving force when vision is blurred or blinded.**
   a. pietistic
   b. unrealistic
   c. exciting
   d. truly optimistic
   e. crippling

Now describe some dream you have had for yourself which remains unfulfilled.

_____

_____

_____

_____

_____

Next, briefly complete the following fantasy diary entry.

**"Dear Diary,
Today I did something entirely new and different.** _____

_____

_____

_____

_____

_____

_____

_____

Discuss with the group your answers to the first five statements. Be sure to supply reasons for each of your choices. Listen carefully to each person's choices and reasons. When you have finished, share your answers to both the question on your unfulfilled dream and the fantasy diary entry.

11 *Entering Life's Spiral*

We enter the spiral when we acknowledge the complexity within ourselves. If we really listen to our heart and our spirit and our imaginings and our dreams and our minds and our bodies, we can no longer cram ourselves into the circumscribed roles or "parts" we are given to play or choose to act out in life.

Socrates challenged the conformity and blindness of Athens, not because he was a revolutionary or a rebel, but simply because he was seeking to be in harmony with himself. He felt that, even if he had to disagree with the whole world, it would be better for him to do so than to be out of harmony with himself. Within himself, Socrates kept finding questions and contradictions which kept moving him on. He took the struggles of his own mind and heart and spirit seriously, and he carried on conversations within himself. The conversations moved him forward. He stopped pretending he had it all together and began to talk about what was going on within him. Thus he became a threat to the status quo.

Dee told me that for many years she responded to life like Pavlov's dog. When someone held up a flag, she saluted. When someone held up a cross, she bowed down. It was crisis that awakened her to the differing voices and pulls and conflicts within her.

It took many years for her to come to peace with the community of voices within herself. She has slowly come to accept her own complexity and even to rejoice in it. She admits now that "I am a mass of contradictions." And she adds playfully, "Is everyone, I hope?"

I once gave a talk describing what I believe are three basic positions in life. The first is the secure circle. This is the position of having a firm and secure place to stand but of being enclosed in its limiting context. The second is that of freedom from the circle. This is the position of someone who has moved out of the secure context but is still existing in a great deal of ambiguity. The third is the entrance into life's spiral. This is the position of being a part of the *process* of living. The process is one of integration, transition, and reintegration.

After the talk, a young man in the audience remarked that he had experienced the first two stages and had a hint of what the third stage was all about, but he placed himself firmly in the second stage. Then he made a very insightful statement. "Whenever I go to work, though, I feel as if there is a great big vacuum sucking me back into position one!"

Many of us have probably felt that kind of pull when we have gone home to visit our parents. We may even start acting like children again. Past contexts have an overwhelming pull on us. Something in them and something in us act as magnets. This is especially true if we are uncertain or shaky about our choices. Then we will tend to revert to where we felt safer. Jesus was expressing a warning to his disciples when he told them to be in the world but not of it. He was moving them into new contexts and was providing for them a strengthened sense of self. "He

who is in you is stronger than he who is in the world."
(*I John* 4:4)

The only way to break free of former contexts which threaten to suck us back is to take the steps which lead to the discovery and creation of new contexts. Then we have more than one place to stand, more than one set of choices, and old contexts slowly lose their power to overtake us.

If we are not taking steps forward, we get pulled back. This going back causes us to feel miserable.

Frank was a man who knew the pull of former contexts. He has been brought up a Seventh Day Adventist. He felt guilty when he was not doing something useful and productive. "I can't stand prosperity," he said. "When things are going well, something inside eats away at me."

Frank had been married and divorced, and the anger and pain — the guilt — of the divorce were still with him. All those feelings flooded back on him when his daughter married and his former wife refused to let him give the bride away. Frank went into a deep depression.

He started getting headaches. After some time, it became apparent that those headaches were linked both to the trauma and what was happening to him in his work. The job he had was intolerable. He really needed to move on. But he felt guilty about letting his fellow workers down. And the thought of *not* working threatened him.

The only thing he had ever really wanted to do was fish. During his career, he had obtained a commercial license, and he owned a boat. He then met a woman who wanted to be a real partner for Frank — a relationship quite different from his first marriage. She and some of his friends encouraged him to do what he really wanted to do. So Frank began to fish for a living.

The feelings of guilt began to pass as Frank got caught up in a new relationship and a new way of life. During the fishing season, he fishes. Off season, he does carpentry. The anger, anxiety, and fear all entered with Frank into a spiral of new activity and hope. Soon those feelings, too, began to fade.

Now Frank has time to read and to pursue lifelong interests. He has more time for celebrating. He has even found that he has a real gift of sharing himself with others and healing others.

Occasionally, Frank's old feelings and depressions return, but usually his life is so taken up with real interests that the feelings soon go away.

Frank sees the past contexts as stages along the way — places he had to leave and move from. The thought of returning is impossible for him to entertain. The moves were necessary. The more he moved into the spiral of new pursuits, the less the past ate away at him. Even the anger and depression — the sense of failure and even the headaches — painful as they were, can now be seen in a positive light. They moved him on.

Former contexts are understood, and the people in them — including ourselves — forgiven, only when we become free of the power which former contexts exert over us. We can gain that freedom when we have found other places to stand and other people to stand with — only when we have entered the spiral. Entering that spiral, we begin to breathe the air of freedom.

RESPONSE

Describe a secure world that you once inhabited. Describe it briefly but with some detail. It should be a secure world that you are now out of.

Now, write how it feels to be out of that secure world. (If you still feel caught, describe how you think it will feel when you are free of that secure world.)

_____

_____

_____

_____

_____

_____

Now describe any steps which you feel will help you enter the spiral of new contexts and new relationships. How will these draw you forward?

_____

_____

_____

_____

_____ ı _____

_____

Finally, list at least three things that might suck you back into the old contexts.

_____

_____

_____

If you can do so comfortably, discuss this with your group. Listen to the similarities of feeling and even some of the same expressions that crop up. There is a great deal of human solidarity in leaving old, secure worlds and getting caught up in new contexts.

12 *Moving Through Many Contexts*

Entering the spiral does not mean running away from one context after another. Nor does it mean jumping without feeling from one relationship or task to the next. Entering the spiral means freely entering a place where you are totally open to life—to all the possibilities of breaking out of your own circles and breaking into those of other people. It can make you at home between different worlds of meaning.

Dorothy Day is a dramatic example of a woman who has lived a life "in-between." She has brought a number of contexts together in her own life. She has opened out new choices not only for herself but for others as well.

Dorothy was visiting friends in San Francisco just after she had been released from jail. She had been arrested for marching with the farmworkers' union in an illegal protest. At the time she was seventy-four.

"That was one of the nicest jails I've ever been in," she told her friends. "The people I met there were so understanding and the accommodations were really nice."

The woman was almost completely free of anger at those whose viewpoints were so desperately different from her own. She was strong in her own convictions, but she did not draw lines or keep others out. Her own journey had taken her through many circles. Throughout her life's journey, however, she had managed to keep an understanding of all the circles within her.

She had grown up middle class. "I am still middle class," she said, "and I will never be anything but middle class. Even the second hand clothes people give me are too nice. I can't really be poor."

Dorothy became a communist in her youth. She was convinced that society needed a radical overturning. She has never abandoned that conviction. But she found that communism lacked spirituality. Her spiritual search led her to enter the Catholic Church. Dorothy was a radical and strong leader. She entered a Church that was in no sense ready for her. All of a sudden she found herself misunderstood by both communists and Catholics.

Dorothy had been a successful journalist, but she left the world of profit-making journalism and started a newspaper (*The Catholic Worker*) with a hand-cranked copy machine. The newspaper sold for a penny. Fifty years later, it still sells for a penny.

Dorothy Day is convinced that society's basic error is the coveting and hoarding of bread, knowledge, technical skill, health care and the like. She believes that to be truly human, people need to share, not accumulate. She sees this as the basic message of Christianity.

To cultivate that sharing, she opened houses to feed the hungry and give shelter to the sick, alcoholic, and the outcast. New York City, like the Church, never knew quite what to do with her. But they didn't know what to do with the hungry either; so they finally gave her a restaurant permit.

Dorothy remains a Catholic communist, a middle class person identified with the poor, a journalist who is not commercial. When she felt called to be somewhere and found no room, she made room. She opened space where people from many different circles have gathered. She dreamed of a world where the closed circles opened up—a world without hatred, prejudice, poverty or war.

Dorothy has a deep conviction that life's spiral does not end in death, but opens out to the greatest possibilities of all. She sees a much greater world beyond the little worlds we live in. She believes in a Spirit which breaks in on our own little worlds and calls us beyond them.

Perhaps most significant, Dorothy is refreshingly free of any exaggerated sense of her own importance. She sees importance everywhere—in every life—in every person—little tugs, or calls which break in from beyond and call us to a different future.

RESPONSE

Whether you are familiar with Dorothy Day or not, write a brief reaction to this description of her. How does this story make you feel?

_____

_____

_____

_____

_____

Dorothy Day experienced a restlessness. Describe one or two areas in your life that make you feel restless. Why do you feel this way?

Reflect for a moment. Is there anything that you feel called to do in the future? It needn't be monumental. If there is, describe what it is and why you feel called to do it.

List some of the different worlds that you bridge or could bridge. Remember that they need not be news-worthy bridges— just real for you.

Spend some time in the group discussing your dreams for the future. Is there a dimension in your dreams that is unselfish? What causes this dimension to keep cropping up?

13 _Putting the Unlikely Together_

In the opening scene of Fedrico Fellini's film, "8½", Guido is caught in the middle of eight lanes of crawling traffic. The smog is oppressive. All the drivers are staring straight ahead. They are all as separate and as alienated from one another as are their cars. Guido coughs, gasps for air, grabs his throat and slumps to the floor of his car. He seems to be choking to death. Suddenly, Guido is catapulted from his car. He flies through the air and lands on a beach. There, he is on location, directing a film.

It soon becomes apparent that Guido cannot pull his life together. There are too many contradictions within him— too much pulling. His wife, his mistress, the Church, his career, his devotion to art, his zany appetite for the bizarre —he cannot reconcile any of them. Guido ends up paralyzed — unable to make decisions about his life or his work.

At the end of the film, Guido's paralysis is resolved in a spectacular fantasy scene. The circus is the event that draws all the disparate elements of Guido's life together for one great celebration. Guido hugs both his wife and his mistress. He kisses the Cardinal's ring. Everyone and everything is there—no longer out of place. Guido shouts, "I need you all!"

Creativity consists in putting unlikely elements together to create effective surprise — the sort of surprise which makes an explosion of recognition inside us and makes us say, "Yes, of course!"

Jerome S. Bruner in his book, *On Knowing — Essays for the Left Hand*, describes effective surprise.

It may express itself in one's dealing with children, in making love, in carrying on a business, in formulating a physical theory, in painting a picture . . . Surprise is not easily defined. It is the unexpected that strikes one with wonder or astonishment. What is curious about effective surprise is that it need not be rare or infrequent or bizarre, and is often none of these things. Effective surprises seem rather to have the quality of obviousness about them when they occur, producing a shock of recognition following which there is no longer astonishment.

The art of living seems to demand this sort of creativity — the blending of unlikely elements into a surprising whole which is unique, deeply human, and beautiful. People who grow create a story of their own which blends unlikely elements and creates effective surprise.

Norm is the personification of effective surprise. The conventional and the unconventional blend together in him as he moves freely from circle to circle. A business failure in the early seventies broke into his secure circle. As he stood free examining what had gone wrong, he was drawn into a number of unlikely circles.

Picture a common scene in the waning days of the Vietnam war. At the naval yards in San Diego, a number of young protestors have positioned themselves to demonstrate against the sending of another aircraft carrier to In-

Creating A New Story 95

dochina. The protestors are a scruffy lot — jeans, beards, backpacks, stringy hair, signs and posters.

Onto the wharf pulls a taxi. From the taxi emerges an impeccably dressed man in a three-piece suit. He is not a lawyer advising the protestors of their rights. He is a stockbroker from San Francisco. Norm has arrived to join the protest.

Anyone can understand how the young people got to that point of protest, but how did Norm get there? He looks back to a business failure as the beginning of his putting the unlikely together.

I had never been with a company that had failed. All at once, with no power to prevent it, I was part of a failing company. The failure really shook me. I think it changed me. After the company went under, I felt, "Well, what's the worst that can happen to me? I can lose everything."

There is something very liberating — very expanding — in being able to say that. That possibility had a tremendous effect on me. I realized that I could survive. I looked at what had happened. I was really out in space. I was blaming myself. I had never really failed before. I zigged when I should have zagged.

But the world didn't stop. My head didn't fall off. Before that, I believed that if I would make the wrong decision, I would have had it.

Actively protesting the war was a growth from that experience. I was tired of lying back and trying not to fail. One day I thought, "This war is wrong, and what am I doing about it? Writing letters to my congressmen isn't enough."

Norm freed himself from an image that had always plagued him. He had felt that, as a businessman, he could not afford to fail or make big mistakes.

Once I set myself free, it wasn't that hard to travel to San Diego to stop an aircraft carrier from going to Vietnam. That was a good experience for me and for the young people there. They couldn't believe someone from the straight community would be interested in expressing unity with their cause—or with them as people. When I arrived in a taxi with my business suit, I actually heard some of them say, "*He* is here to *help* us?"

After the protest, Norm moved seriously into other contexts. He had always loved music. He organized people from the Bay Area Cursillo (Little Course in Christianity) community to give concerts. The group produced a successful recording.

World hunger bothered him. He began thinking about hunger. His response was to put two ideas together in a very unlikely way. He organized and produced "Concerts for the Hungry." The proceeds from this effort went to organizations directly involved with feeding the hungry.

Norm is still a stockbroker on Montgomery Street. But Norm is also a musician, a radical, a believer and a politician. As all these things he confuses people. In the various circles in which he travels, he causes quiet consternation. But from deep within himself there is the peace that comes from being where he knows he is called to go.

Today, Norm is still a person on the move. He is still probing the future — still looking for a way to put the unlikely together.

Lately my dreams are telling me something about what direction I should go in. I see my dreams as a kind of an indication. I am always looking for direction because I never feel that anything I'm doing is necessarily what I'm going to end up doing. I am always stepping toward something else. That is what makes my life interesting — entering that mystery of what's next and penetrating the darkness.

People who create effective surprises — who make their own story — are no longer bound by the walls of separation and convention around them. They unite the opposites in themselves and so move in and out of the various contexts around them without being imprisoned by any one of them.

RESPONSE

This section is a chance for you to play with all the unlikely contexts that your life affords. Some of them are only dreams today. Others of them are realities that somehow don't quite fit. Some of them are children whose life styles differ from your own. Others may be skills you have never cultivated. Still others may be responsibilities that you have not been able to face. Perhaps you no longer know just how faith or religion fits into your life. Maybe you want to take action to right some wrong that exists in society. You may even want to heal an old wound or search for some spiritual depth. One evening Jacob of the Old Testament wrestled with an angel. He engaged in quite a battle. It went on for hours like some barroom brawl in a vintage western movie. But when the wrestling was over, Jacob knew the spot where this struggle took place was indeed holy ground.

The Response in this section is not a brawl, but it is important. When you are through with this exercise, the place where you did this dreaming can really be called "holy ground."

Use the blank spaces in the columns below to help you get started. On each line write down a dream or an image of yourself. Write anything that you can or want to see yourself doing.

Include everything: Tahiti, golf, love, skills, playful things, painful things, powerful things. Just jot.

_____	_____	_____
_____	_____	_____
_____	_____	_____
_____	_____	_____
_____	_____	_____
_____	_____	_____
_____	_____	_____
_____	_____	_____
_____	_____	_____
_____	_____	_____
_____	_____	_____
_____	_____	_____

Now, take a deep breath and take lots of paper—one sheet for every idea you have on those lines. Write the idea on the top of the page and start to play. Take time, enjoy it. When you have written ideas on every page and have thought about each idea, spread the papers out on the floor. Get a mosaic impression of your dreams and images. (If you are working in a group, move into all available space. Posture and decorum are not necessary because you are putting the unlikely together.)

- What predominates in your dreams and images?
- Are there any unlikely combinations?
- Sort the dreams into groups—playful images, work dreams, relationship dreams, etc.
- What group is the largest and the strongest?
- Does all this give you any indication of the kind of balance you might be called to?

- Does all this give you a better picture of yourself?
- Pick from the ideas, dreams, and images those which you most want to realize. Indicate which are pure fantasy.
- How many of these are possible?

When you have settled down, discuss with the group just how you felt when you were going through this exercise. Share those dreams which suddenly seemed more real. Share those difficult situations which do not seem so difficult anymore. Let people see how you enter the spiral.

14 *Meeting Monsters Along the Way*

The greatest obstacles to the creation of a new story are monsters. Some of these monsters are conjured up from our own past, others roar at us from the society all around us. These monsters can have tremendous power over us. They can (if we let them) determine the direction of our lives.

Everywhere, along the way, the monsters rear up and scream: "Stop! Go Back! Freeze! NO! You Can't! Back to the secure world!" Whether the monsters are within us or outside and no matter what form they take, they are all forms of fear or threat. This fear can paralyze us and make us cower. And the fear can send us back to where we came from.

The monsters come in the form of faces from the past— peering over the shoulder and watching over every move. They shake their heads in disapproval. Once when I felt paralyzed by those faces, I turned and pictured each one and stared at it. As I stared at each face in turn, I noted the pinched look of fear, unhappiness, and insecurity. I asked myself, "Do I really want *these* faces to control my life?"

Other monsters cry warning, "You will not know the way if you venture ahead. You will be lost." They try to convince us not to move unless we have the whole course mapped out in advance. They use the tactics of separation. "Certainly not a woman of your background ..." "Not at your age. It is too late." "That is no way for a sane person to live."

Everyone has flaws in his or her background. We move on, not because of what has been our background, but in spite of it. As for age? When is too old to change? There is a story about the woman who told her psychiatrist that she didn't want to go back to school to finish her degree because when she finished, she would be fifty. "And if you don't get your degree," the psychiatrist responded, "how old will you be then?" After all, at any age, is it more sane to refuse growth or change than it is to embrace it?

Perhaps the most threatening of the monsters is the fear of loneliness. "If you move ahead, you will be left alone. Others will not understand. You will have no one."

It is true that some steps need to be taken alone. But there is a further truth: You will be met. Sometimes others are already where you are headed. You may have to seek them out. You may need to show yourself before they appear. But as the saying goes, "When the student is ready, the master appears." When the beloved is open and alive, the lover appears.

The fear of loneliness, the fear of loss, the allure of security over risk, all these are the voices of the past. They make their din in an attempt to drown out the cry of the future within us. They try to cause static so that we will not hear the call from beyond. In the words of Nikos Kazantzakis, "I call in despair, 'Where can I go? I have reached the pinnacle. Beyond is the abyss.' And the Cry answers, 'I am beyond. Stand up.'" (*Report to Greco*)

Ben, the alcoholic you met in Part Two, discovered the process at an Alcoholics Anonymous meeting.

One night some guy at the meeting spoke of his anguish over coming to some decision. He said he heard in the midst of his pain, "Be still and hear my voice." I think that comes as close to being a description of prayer as anything I know. You have to get free—free from all the entanglements of an active mind, from all the fear and anxiety. Some of the toughest decisions (and this guy's was tough) seem to me to have been made by being quiet—by somehow getting loose from all the oppressive, dismaying, despair inducing aspects of a problem. Sit still and pray that what you are to do will be made clear to you.

RESPONSE

First of all, in the four squares below, draw some of your monsters.

Now, on the lines below, write down some of the things your monsters are telling you to do or not to do. (If you are working in a group, you may want to act this part out.)

_____

_____

_____

_____

_____

_____

_____

Now spend some time in meditation. Focus on an area in your life where you need guidance. Consciously flick the monsters away from you until you can, "Be still and hear my voice." You can use the space below to doodle about what you hear. Do not feel the compulsion to write anything, however. The first task is to listen.

Share some of your monsters with the group. Let the others in on what you fear most about the path you are on. Why do you have these fears? Listen to how the group feeds back to you on your fears.

15 *The Final Crisis*

Meeting life's crises differently may well be a preparation for meeting death differently. Over the past twenty years, there has been a great deal of research with the dying. People who face death fear darkness, oblivion, or aloneness. Interviews with people who had been clinically dead and then were revived have uncovered a remarkable pattern.

Those who experienced clinical death met light, not darkness. They entered not oblivion but a higher state of awareness. They did not feel alone. They were met by others who loved them. Perhaps most significant, they were less afraid to die again.

On the other side of crisis (when that crisis is faced with creativity) is light. People who have entered into the experience have grown to a new awareness. Even though those people took very lonely steps, they were met by loving and raring people. And people who have creatively faced crisis are not afraid to face crisis again.

Perhaps the crises of life — the disintegrations and reintegrations—are all a preparation for the great letting go in death. For those who have entered the spiral, possibilities open up, even in death.

Bill was a tough police inspector in a large city. He was a very unlikely teacher of death's possibilities. Bill's life had taken him through a number of transitions. He had had many experiences which plunged him into the grimmer aspects of reality. He once observed, "There is hardly a block in this city that does not remind me of some horrible thing that happened there."

For a time Bill gave lie detector tests. When he was young he would meet important people in the city — politicians, judges, clergy, presidents of corporations — and would be nervous in the presence of their greatness. But after giving lie detector tests to all sorts of people, he said, "Now, when I meet somebody important, I can't help but think in the back of my head, 'I wonder if this person is some sort of crook!'"

Bill's job filled him with a great deal of cynicism. But over the years he moved beyond that and began looking for something constructive that he could do. Although he had been brought up in the deep South, he joined actively in the civil rights movement. Both the police force and the parish to which he belonged ridiculed him a bit for his stands on justice for black people. He finally had to leave the parish because of the ridicule of the parish priest and some prominent members of the community there.

Bill became more and more involved in promoting justice for those who hadn't had much of a chance in life. A fellow police officer reported that Bill would stop in the middle of an investigation or a lie detector test and have a heart to heart talk with the suspect. "This isn't turning out well for you. Do you want to try to do something about that? I know a few judges, and while I can't guarantee anything, if you want to talk, I can work to get you a fair shake."

Bill looked around for a long time to find some people who really needed him. He concluded that the deaf were some of the most neglected people in society. He gave much of his time to the deaf. He found jobs for them. In one case he trained a group of them for employment with the Post Office. He helped the deaf when they were arrested or were in the courts. In Bill the deaf of the city had ears.

He was in his mid-fifties when he learned that he had cancer. He knew he was going to die, and he wanted to do it in a way that was good for his family and friends.

At the deaf center where Bill went to church, he talked to people about his death. "When you find out you're going to die, it's all right. The only regrets I have are that I got a little late start in life doing the things I really want to do. I know that you will carry them on. You are great people, and I love you."

Bill wanted to die at home. Once, when a friend came to call on him, Bill's wife went to pour a drink. She discovered that they were out of bourbon. From the bedroom came a voice, "If you go downstairs in the garage and reach behind the two-by-four in the corner, you'll find a bottle. You'll also find forty dollars, which was to be for your birthday present. Those are all my secrets, and after thirty-five years of marriage, I think that's a pretty good record!"

Bill received a stream of visitors. He took everyone of them through his death. He told them that he was going to die and that he felt all right about it. He took *them* beyond his death. Then he would talk with them, telling them the things he had always wanted to say to them. They would see their own lives through Bill's eyes. Sometimes they would leave in tears. Most often they would leave in joy because they were filled with a sense of possibility.

Bill planned his own funeral. He knew what he wanted.

He wanted his hands crossed over his chest in the casket. He wanted them to form the deaf sign for the word *love*. Love beyond death. His funeral was to be held in a gym where the deaf people met. Since Bill had brought people through his death beforehand, much of the grieving was finished beforehand as well. As a result, his funeral was a celebration. In his dying the words of Saint Paul had real meaning, "Death, where is your victory? Where is your sting?"

Raymond, an elderly deaf man who died not too long after Bill, described his impending death this way: "I am going to join the spirit of Bill Hamlet."

In entering the last crisis, Bill was able to say that in death as in life, "It is all right. Don't be afraid. Go ahead!"

RESPONSE

Spend a few moments in silence. Unite yourself with the spirits of those who have passed through crisis before you. Listen to their wisdom—discovered as it was on the paths through crisis. Try to apply that wisdom to your life. After a few moments, write down the one thought that strikes you most strongly during your reflection.

When you feel ready, try to picture your life from some still point in your future and look back from that point. On the lines of the spiral on the following page, jot down the key words that describe what you see.

Bill thought he got a late start doing the things he really wanted to do. List three things you really want to do with the rest of your life. What holds you back?

1. _____

2. _____

3. _____

In the group, share how you really feel about death. Do you see it as the ultimate crisis? Do you feel that the way you have handled other crises in your life can help you with your death?

PART FIVE

Picturing the Process

You can take life on as a heavy burden ... or as part of the dance.

—RAM DASS

Those who learn the most from crisis become more and more flexible. They are free to move in many different directions. They no longer see themselves as finished products whose roles in life are set and determined.

People who have passed through the pain of personal crisis have found a way beyond anything they had previously known. They have begun to live in new ways. Yet they know that there are other ways even beyond what they have discovered — other choices they have yet to dream of.

This book now contains a picture of you—of your paths through crisis. Because you have entered the pages of this book, you have already taken some significant steps. This last part of the book is a reflection on the whole. It is a chance for you to review and to celebrate what is happening in your life because the words and pictures present steps which do not tell *a* person's story. They tell *all* people's story. Every man and woman who has faced major crisis and has been unable to accept the alternatives available has passed through the steps. In one sense, the words and the pictures — the steps — make up a "folk dance" because the steps are steps which real people have taken in their lives. They trace the process of human beings at their best as they move through change.

Although the images focus upon major crisis and personal growth, they work for any number of quandaries in life from moving, to finding a job, to buying a house, to dealing with relationships, to choosing what sort of foods to eat, to changing lifestyle patterns.

PREVIEW

As you go through the last part of the book, place yourself in the images as you go through them. Feel free to use them for different areas in *your* life. To prepare for this, answer the following questions briefly. The questions are designed to remind you of those things in this book which are most important for you and which you can use in this process.

1. What were the two most significant things you read or did while going through this book? Why were they important?

   a. _____

   _____

   _____

   b. _____

   _____

   _____

2. How do you feel about yourself right now?

   _____

   _____

   _____

   _____

   _____

3. Describe one thing you feel now that gives you hope for your future.

   _____

   _____

   _____

   _____

   _____

   _____

4. Describe one thing that makes you fearful.

_____

_____

_____

_____

_____

5. Describe in a few sentences how you intend to progress in your life.

_____

_____

_____

_____

_____

_____

Now go on to picture the process. The dance described in the following pages can be handled in many ways. Read through it quickly. Read through it slowly. Feel free to jot down next to the pictures the times and places when this was you. Make note of the steps you have not taken. See what images you cannot yet identify with. They might suggest possibilities. Feel free to talk about what you see. In fact, sharing your feelings can help you uncover alternatives, contexts and possibilities.

Only one caution. The little people pictured here are not an exact mirror of reality. They cannot tell you what to do. The people in this dance are simply handy to have around. Consult them whenever you go through a process of change and human decision.

CIRCLES OF SECURITY

People grow up and live at least part of their adult lives *encircled*. They do not realize they are encircled, because they do not *see* the rims of the circles.

The circle is roughly equivalent to "the way things are." It is seen not as *a* context, but as *the* context.

Choices are possible, but they are limited to those envisioned within the circle. Different ways of relating are possible, but they are confined to ways that are acceptable within the circle.

Remaining within the circle is remaining within sanity, within humanity. Like maps of old, uncharted areas outside the circle might contain the warning, "Beyond here there be dragons."

DRIFTING

The positive side of circles—personal, familial, cultural—is that they nourish and protect life. People grow up within them. To grow up "outside" any circle would be to be without a family, a culture, a background, a name.

The negative side of circles is their limiting and narrowing effect. To remain within one circle is to be confined to first-order or "zero" learning, learning *things* within a context.

People who remain confined to the same circle become drifters and decisions are made *for* them.

The drifter "has not yet found himself." And so he is content to choose what everyone else is choosing. But the others, too, are apt to be drifters, each of them doing and choosing and thinking and saying what others happen to be doing and choosing and thinking and saying.

When confined to a circle, one is constantly held down by the heaviness of this world and is unable to do other than repeat the same full round over again.

Politically and socially, to remain fixed within a "circle of certainty" is to have a "fatalistic perception of the universe" and a "sectarian" mentality.

CRISIS

People become aware of their encirclement when they experience crisis. What used to work for them no longer works. What felt good before now becomes uncomfortable or even unbearable.

Sometimes crisis breaks in from the outside. Sometimes it erupts from within. It makes a painful opening in a circle which was formerly closed and secure.

People begin to feel trapped by the reality around them. They try to escape, but cannot. The more they face their predicament, the more painful it becomes. And they are afraid.

"I was going through the hardest thing, also the greatest thing for any human being to do—to accept that which is already within you and around you." (*Malcolm X*).

DILEMMA OR THE END OF CHOICES

Severe pain is caused whenever someone faces a crisis for which he can find no acceptable solution. In such a case one can no longer tolerate his arena of choices; yet there is nowhere to go.

Such an experience is paralyzing and fraught with the danger of depression, psychosis, or simply "adjusting" (settling for what seems possible within the circle—a living death).

TRANSITION

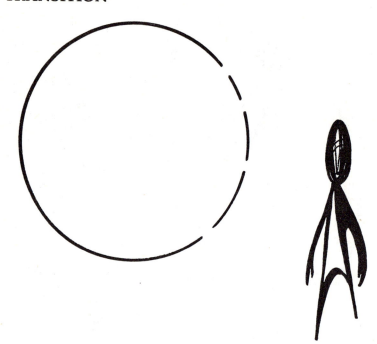

Continuing to deal with impossible choices can slowly move people out of the context to which they have been confined. They can take small, groping steps which slowly lead them to a place beyond the alternatives formerly available **to** them.

The steps seem insignificant at the time, but they are the beginnings of following the true self, the deepest insides, the "Cry Within."

VULNERABILITY

The period "in-between," when former patterns are no longer working and new patterns are not yet formed, is a very vulnerable time. People deal with aloneness, despair and "ex-communication." If they look to past standards for judgments of themselves, they are continually found guilty. (The individuals and groups they formerly related to often do not understand them and consider them "problems" or threats.) The people themselves do not "have it together." They do not make sense to themselves, and the world does not make sense to them. They often feel they are screwed up, misfits, failures. They know what they do *not* want much more than what they do want.

Being in touch with someone who loves and accepts and forgives and encourages is crucial at this time.

ACCEPTANCE OF BEING INTERIM

Little by little people can learn to live with ambiguity, with not knowing what to do, with being interim.

It is important during this period *not to demand* a final solution. If people persist in demanding final solutions, they often end up exchanging the circle they left behind for another one just like it.

To remain interim means moving step by step without yet having a master plan. The necessity of groping one's way is pointed out by Bateson: "It is the very nature of exploring not to know beforehand that which is being explored."

FEELING ONE'S WAY

People begin to try things, to take steps that are tentative, sometimes erratic. They no longer move "rationally" (by the reasonableness of a former context) but rather by getting in touch with and beginning to follow their deepest insides.

Following out hunches, intuitions, images and dreams becomes important.

Like the man who was given up for lost in the blizzard and survived, people can say of themselves in this period, "I just took one step and then another."

THE SELF BECOMING A COMMUNITY

Listening to the different centers of the self and allowing them to be in touch with each other is extremely important. The body speaks its mind. Feelings (and stored energy) erupt. Dreams and imaginings unfold. There is a possibility for imagination and feeling and thought and dream to become engaged in fruitful interplay, for the self to become a community of voices.

Feeling and thinking reactions are no longer clearly separated from each other. Mind and heart and imagination and action and relationship begin to have an on-going reciprocal influence on each other. The different centers of the self are in fruitful tension and begin to point out directions to take.

INTEGRATION

There arise periods of new integration — "having it together for now"—which are encouraging. People begin to benefit from the value of hindsight, of seeing where they have moved and for the first time getting an outside look at the context they have left behind. They realize where they have been. They do not want to go back. And they begin to sense new relationships, a new set of alternatives and new patterns forming for them. A trust in the *process* develops.

A NEW FORM OF EQUILIBRIUM

Whereas previously, equilibrium was maintained by "standing firm" within a circle, balance is now maintained only by ongoing responsive movement. Security no longer comes from standing still and controlling the outside world; security comes from ongoing response to persons, events and inner experience. Ways of responding are not determined beforehand, but become apparent only along the way.

A way of proceeding emerges which eventually incorporates past patterns and continues to develop new ones. Flexibility grows. A slow spiralling process continues which leaves open the possibility for ongoing transformation.

CO-RELATING

Relationships change. People who have been controlling begin to let go of their need to control others for their purposes. Those who have been controlled begin to feel their own being and their own power.

People are met by others who sense and appreciate and accept their journey. Relationships are no longer determined by ties within past circles.

There is a new sharing of the depths of the self. Love and understanding and challenge and weakness are shared. For some, purpose begins to be less important than love. For a few, there is a great letting go.

FREEDOM AND FLEXIBILITY

By moving beyond their own set patterns and the limitations of past contexts, people experience freedom. New sets of alternatives open out for them. They become capable of living in a number of contexts, and no one of the contexts defines who they are. They have a constant sense that there *is* more than is presently apparent to them.

Reality no longer is experienced as confining. Set ways of acting (inner compulsions) are no longer necessary to "control" the outside world.

LIVING FROM THE FUTURE

Past circles are no longer seen as closed but as parts of the spiral. Meeting and parting, entering and leaving, beginning and ending are seen as necessary parts of the journey, stages along the way. Love melts the walls that separate and divide and judge. The past no longer has determining power. The cry of the future can now be heard.

People sense the unexpected as possible and so begin to live their lives as if the future already existed. The cry of the future can draw them on, and symbols from the past can take on new meaning and give indications of a different future.

"Be still and hear my Voice."

CREATIVITY

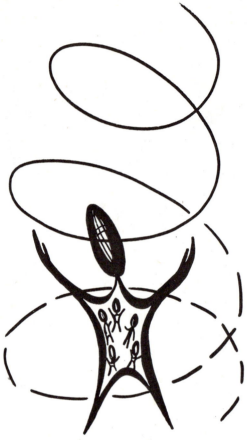

Areas of the self which had been blocked now become free to express themselves. Conscious and unconscious, thought and feeling, past and present begin to come together. The experience of a number of different contexts opens combinations of possibilities.

It becomes possible to "wear many hats," to combine in our lives a number of unlikely elements to produce "effective surprise" There is a fresh excitement and unpredictability to life. There is an opportunity to put together the new.

OTHERS EMERGING

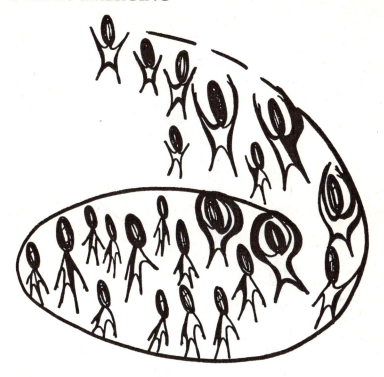

When some individuals act and begin to create their own stories, they open a way for others. Their lives communicate a sense of *possibility* and beckon to others who are close to turning points.

People sense that others exist and still others are emerging—others who have moved beyond personal compulsions and group "isms." The hope and sanity and survival of the planet depends on such an emergence.

THE CRITICAL POINT

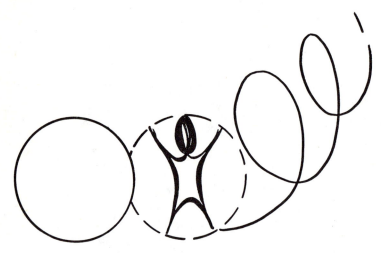

There is no elite. No one ever *arrives*. The critical point reappears in every life. There is no secret way, no completed creation, no ultimate revolution, no top of the tower.

The point of the Babel story in the Bible is that there can be no authentic human structure reaching to the heavens. Such a structure, be it communist or Catholic, humanist or utopian, would stifle the development of the human spirit. The tower has no top.

The critical point is never transcended in this life. Only movement to break through all that threatens to finish the human spirit can be hopeful. The only way to keep freedom and creativity alive is to constantly *exercise* freedom and to *choose* alternatives.

BEYOND EXPERIENCES

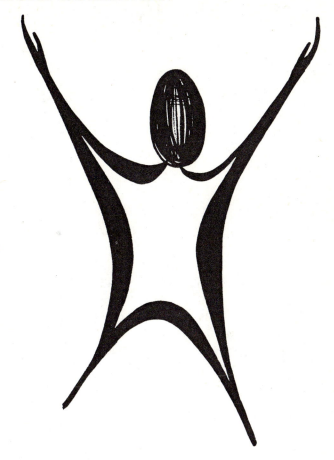

For some there are, along the way, experiences of the circles melting away, a moving beyond subjectivity and objectivity to a great feeling of Oneness. There are moments of ecstasy and enlightenment, "letting mind and body fall."

The "Cry Within" and the "Cry Without" become one. People regain a child-like wonder and enter the Mystery. They experience Love at the heart of Reality.

Conclusion

. . . Unless a man be born again . . .he cannot enter the kingdom.

—GOSPEL OF JOHN

. . . Freedom at least opens out the possibility of something better.
Enslavement is the certainty of the worst.

—ALBERT CAMUS

. . . You are your own masters now . . .

—THE LAST WORDS OF BUDDHA TO HIS DISCIPLES

CELEBRATING THE STEPS ALONG THE WAY

Once I had a dream. I was walking along a barren road with a pair of sandals in my hands. The sandals were old and worn and cracked. I was *eating* them, bite by bite, and it was making me sick. I turned and saw my parents behind me on the road. I walked back to them and said, "It's crazy for me to keep eating my sandals. They're making me sick."

There was a garbage can by the side of the road. I threw my old sandals into it and felt a great relief. That was the end of my dream.

My dream fit my life at the time. The path I had been walking *was* making me sick. It had once been a nourishing path for me, but I was no longer one with it. I was forcing it on myself now, and I could not stomach it. It was making me curse my life.

I left the path I knew. In fear and anxiety, I began taking steps in other directions. I felt bad about myself and had a sense of failure.

I could not see where I was going. I was afraid to take steps because I did not know where they would lead. I needed love and encouragement and understanding. I sought out friends who understood and did not judge. They nourished me and kept me alive.

I began to listen to hunches and suggestions and daydreams. My images began to lead me. Moving along without knowing was uncomfortable, but I began to accept it. I began to try different things, to take steps. I tried to get in touch with the "diviner" within me, the wise man, limping along, not knowing, getting nowhere, and then suddenly running into something — sensing it was right. I began to trust my inner sense of what was right.

Only in retrospect can I understand and appreciate how important those halting steps were. Without them, I might still be back where I was—cursing my life.

Now, I can celebrate those steps. I sensed they were right at the time, even though at the time something nagged at me and made me feel bad about taking them. I have slowly learned to recognize — no matter what my "monsters" tell me — what is a *good* step for me. And I have begun to celebrate even the painful steps—the ones I wish I didn't have to take.

The great human celebrations began with painful steps. The steps of Abraham, of people in the desert, of Jesus in agony. It's easy to celebrate those old steps as feasts now. They seem so clean and detached from the human struggle. But it isn't easy to celebrate our own journeys. And yet, if we don't celebrate steps we are taking *now*, we can forget how significant they really are and stop taking them.

Recently we had a Seder Meal which focused not on the journey of the Jewish people, but on our own journeys. The people present shared what they were leaving and what they were going towards, what their slavery and their freedom involved.

Some had difficulties talking about their own steps; some tended to underestimate them. But in the eyes of the group, each journey was great. Agony and ecstasy, death and rising, hope and possibility were present in each person, and there was a sense that something was happening in us which was shaking the earth just a little bit!

Recently, a friend of mine gave a different kind of party. He invited only people who were making hard human decisions, who were taking steps and struggling to be true to themselves. There was a sense at that party of people in touch with themselves—people in vital contact with life, who in reaching inside themselves had found a source beyond themselves. That source which Buddhists call the Buddha-nature, which Hindus call the Universal Self, and which Christians recognize as the Spirit of God at the heart of humanity.

Old Ben told me that years ago he began to sense possibility all around him, in a wink here and a handshake there, in all different sorts of people, glimmerings of possibility and promise. Little echoes of a Voice deep within the human spirit which says, "We will not go back. We will keep going!"